30 Day Ketogenic Vegetarian Meal Plan

The Essential Ketogenic Vegetarian Diet for Beginners – 30 Days Ketogenic Vegetarian Meal Prep (Lose up to 30 Pounds in 30 Days)

Virginia Brewer

Table of contents

Introduction

From the early age, we all are taught to eat sugars for energy and that it is the primary source of energy. However, there is another fuel, much more efficient and health friendly known as ketones.

A brief introduction of ketones is that when the body burns fat, the result is the release of ketones in the body which are then absorbed by body cells to carry out vital actions in the body. When this happens, meaning when the body switches to the fat burning machine, the body is said to undergo in a state called ketosis. In other words, when the body consumes a high-fat diet, ketosis occurs.

This isn't a new thing. The ketogenic diet was first discovered to treat epilepsy in children. However, with the progress and explosion in the research for this diet, Ketogenic diet has become the life of people. Recent trends in the Ketogenic diet has divided it into types, Ketogenic meat diet, and Ketogenic vegetarian diet.

Now the next question arises that most of the vegetables are high carb so how they can meet the diet requirements of the Ketogenic diet. Well, a brief answer is that the combination of complete knowledge on Ketogenic diet and vegetarian diet, you can smartly come up with meals that not only keep up with the notion of Ketogenic diet but are also delicious.

Read on to know more how.

Chapter 1: Understanding the Ketogenic Diet

The History of Keto

The word Keto became popular in the 20 centuries, somewhere between the 1920s and 1p30s, when a high-fat diet was being adopted to combat the plague of epilepsy. Physicians before that time had no idea to save individuals suffering from epilepsy and were trying every diet as a treatment. They always end up in failure, but they were on right track and that track ended on the destination called Ketogenic diet.

In the 20th century, the physician found a therapy for epilepsy in the form of fasting or more specifically the Ketogenic diet. Even before that time, fasting was observed as a means of treatment for a disease. The first experiment included about 20 subjects suffering from epilepsy. Doctors observed the immediate results of fasting on the subjects in the form of minimized effects of epilepsy due to burning of fat in the body during fasting. As a result, the effect of epilepsy gets significantly reduce in their bodies. And from there, the word spread, and doctors started using this medical breakthrough to improve the epilepsy situation in children. Though fasting was a very effective cure it was not a long-term solution, after all, people require food to live. And hence, fasting transitioned into dieting. People who fasted contains ketones in their bodies, acetone and beta-hydroxybutyric therefore, the permanent solution for epilepsy was the continuous production of ketones in the body. For this, a renowned physician at the Mayo Clinic, Dr. Peterman, present following alteration in the diet which led to the development of the Ketogenic diet.

- 12 to 15 g of carbs per day,
- 1g of proteins per kilogram of body weight,
- And the remaining calories come from fat.

And hence, Ketogenic diet came out as an unquestionable weapon to lead an epilepsy-free life. However, it was until late 20 century when interest in Ketogenic diet revived. In 1994, a two-year-old boy of a Hollywood producer, Jim Abrahams, was suffering from epilepsy. The family pursued every doctor and did every treatment, but everything ended in failure until Jim discovered references of Ketogenic diet to fight epilepsy. His son's condition, under this diet, improved significantly and his epilepsy was controlled. This inspired Abrahams to create awareness of Ketogenic diet and to gather funding for it. He produced a TV movie called "First Do No Harm" and from there began an explosion of interest of common man and scientist in this diet. Not only for the treatment of epilepsy, was the Ketogenic diet under investigation for its other benefits. The popularity of the Ketogenic diet spread through 45 countries by 2007. By the current time, the Ketogenic diet has become one of the hottest diet trends and people are adopting it as a lifestyle.

The Ketosis Process

When the ketone level in blood in above 0.5mmol/L, the metabolic state of the body is called ketosis. The word 'ketosis' is a short form of the word 'Ketogenesis" which means generating ketones. Generating ketones is a natural process our body carries out when carbohydrates are sufficiently low in the body and fats breakdowns for energy, for example after exercise or during fasting. This supply of fat keeps you from starvation.

Why Body Use Ketones?

Normally, the body makes use of stored carbs in the form of glycogen and convert it into simple sugar, glucose. The insulin hormone is secreted into the body that helps blood glucose to get into cells where glucose is further converted into energy called ATP. Now, when there is no more glucose to generate ATP, then fatty acids in the body are oxidized to use as an alternate. This induced ketosis in the body and the by-products are ketones.

So How Do I Know I Am in Ketosis?

Ketosis can be trigger into the body for any of the following reasons:

- Reduced number of calories,
- Reduced amount of carbohydrates and increase amount of fat,
- A long period of intense exercise
- Being pregnant.

You will notice the following symptoms and changes in your body

- Fruity smell or smell similar to a nail polish remover,
- Healthier hairs and skin
- Shortness of breath
- Increase thirst and dry mouth
- Decreased cravings
- Frequent urination
- Fatigue
- Feeling energetic throughout the day
- Lower inflammation
- Mental clarity

The most reliable way to know ketones level is through a urine test and blood test. Urine Keto testing kits are used which comprises Keto sticks on which urine sample is used. If the body is under ketosis, the strip changes its color. Use the guide with the Keto stick to know the level of ketosis by comparing the color change. In the blood test, the ketone level is low if comes under 0.6 mmol/L. Ketone level is considered in the mid-range when falls between 0.6 mmol/L and 1.5 mmol/L. Ketone level above 1.5 mmol/L is considered high.

Benefits of Ketogenic Diet

Though when the Ketogenic diet was discovered, it was strictly used to treat epilepsy in children, however with the progress in the Ketogenic diet, it has become versatile and has many great benefits.

Weight loss: One of the major reason people turn to Ketogenic loss is for weight loss. Ketogenic diet makes body shed weight more quickly compared to other diets. This happens due to the consumption of fat instead of sugar for energy. Weight loss is more if you adapt to exercise in your daily routine. To make sure weight loss goes smoothly, calculate your macros and calorie intake using Keto calculator. A standard Keto calculator recommends 5% carbs, 20% protein and 75% fat in a Ketogenic diet. For this, eat quality full-fat (healthy fats) and low carb food and completely avoid processed food. Most importantly, don't rush into it, you have to give your time to get into ketosis which is usually between 2 to 7 days. Also, keep track of the ketone level. Weight loss ultimately helps with the regulation of hormones and blood sugar levels in the body.

Improved insulin sensitivity: Disturbance in insulin sensitivity leads to diabetes due to increase level of glucose in the blood. To control insulin levels, the Ketogenic diet works best. In the condition of high blood sugar, eating carbohydrate is harmful as it can spike the blood sugar level. Therefore, cutting carbs and turning to a high-fat diet, blood sugar can be reduced. But don't restrict carb too much as it can lead to low blood sugar condition, known as hypoglycemia. Take advice from a doctor when using the Ketogenic diet to treat diabetes.

Improved Mental Focus and Clarity: Most of the time, an unhealthy diet is a reason for the foggy brain, weak memory and lack of focus and mental clarity. These all can be improved with a clean diet like a Ketogenic diet. Actually, every cell in the body needs fat and that to healthy fat and what can be best than a high-fat diet to meet this requirement. Ketones generated using ketosis increased the efficiency of cells in brain and body and boost their energy levels.

Alzheimer's disease: Alzheimer is a devastating disease and very difficult to treat. The brain of individuals suffering from Alzheimer's disease is always in need of fuel and brain is one big muscle. Luckily, use of Ketogenic diet is safe to turn the body into fat instead of carbs for fuel. Not only this, current researches and experiments proved ketones in the body led to improvement in memory, language, and mental focus to complete tasks.

Cancer: Research shows that it is sugar which feeds cancer and led to the development of chronic diseases. Therefore, the Ketogenic diet has come out as a key to recover from cancer. This high-fat diet weakens cancer cell and makes the immune system strong. The lower levels of carbs with the Ketogenic diet reduces the level of glucose in the body and therefore, the cancer cell is unable to get the energy to deplete. Ketogenic diet makes the cancer cell starve for energy which they normally obtain from glucose as they cannot metabolize fatty acids. Ultimately, in the absence of glucose, the survival rate of cancer cell decline significantly and thus, cancer is prevented successfully.

Chapter 2: Vegetarian Basic

What is a Vegetarian Diet?

A vegetarian diet is a meal which excludes meat. Based on the historical document, a vegetarian diet was adopted in parts of the world which is now India and Greece in the 6th century BC. The idea behind to become vegetarian was to unharmed animals, environment, and other health reasons. It was also a belief that eating meat is not the only way to get all the nutrients. At that time, vegetarianism was spread widely in this region and still, vegetarian is strictly practice in Hindu, Jain and Buddhism religion. When the Roman Empire converted to Christianity, vegetarianism got vanish and got revived between 19th and 20th century. Vegetarian societies were formed in England, Germany, and other European countries. It promotes the idea to enjoy a healthy life and to make more active and this led to a rise in vegetarians.

Food in Vegetarian Diet

A vegetarian diet is can be described by what is served for a food. There are five types of vegetarians based on their diet.

1. **Vegans** are vegetarians that do not eat any meat, animal product and their by-products. Their meal is also devoid of dairy, eggs and gelatin items.
2. **Pesci-vegetarian** doesn't eat meat and poultry but consume egg, dairy products, and fish.
3. **Lacto vegetarian** does consume dairy products but avoids eggs, meat, poultry, and fish.
4. **Ovo-vegetarian** eats eggs and doesn't consume meat, poultry, and fish.
5. **Lacto-ovo vegetarians** are the most common type of vegetarians. They eat eggs and dairy product and don't eat meat, poultry, and fish.

Advantages of The Vegetarian Diet

A vegetarian diet is a healthy life. First of all, a great benefit of a vegetarian diet is **conservation of the environment**. According to a study, the environmental impacts of non-vegetarians are more than vegetarians. They consume water more, use fuel more and energy more to arrange their food compared to vegetarians. Studies proved that meat diets create too many strains on the environment, specifically in consuming water. On the other hand, reduce the amount of water, fuel and energy are noted for a vegetarian diet.

Another advantage of a vegetarian diet is **protecting animal life**. Animal killings are gradually increasing which is quicken the pace of extinction. Not only that, an enormous number of animals are slaughtered to meet the high demand for meat by people for food. The increase in population means the more the food so the more killing of animals. In comparison to this, vegetarian eat meat very less which led to less demand for animals and thus, saving the lives of animals.

Most importantly, the vegetarian diet brings **positive impacts on health** by reducing the risk of harmful diseases. The reason is the presence of phytochemicals, a type of anti-oxidant, which is great to fight dangerous ailments. Various research has proved that vegetarianism lowers the risk of chronic diseases like heart diseases, kidney diseases, cancer and diabetes, especially type 2 diabetes. It also helps in controlling high blood pressure and treat obesity by weight loss. Becoming a vegetarian led to healthier and longer life expectancy.

Chapter 3: The Ketogenic Vegetarian Diet
Benefits of The Ketogenic Vegetarian Diet

The ketogenic diet is a versatile diet. It means that it is suitable for a meat lover and also a plant-based food lover.

But how is this possible when Ketogenic when Ketogenic diet normally include a lot of meat in the food to meat protein requirement and cut of vegetables to reduce carbs?

The answer is fat because high quantity of fat is the key component of a Ketogenic diet which can also easily get from vegetarian meals. Plus, it is very easy to go keto while staying from meat and adapting diet with low carb vegetables that also offer plant-based fats. You just have to be little careful to not use high carb vegetables and beans and grains which aren't a part of food list of a Keto diet.

So what to eat and what to avoid in a Ketogenic vegetarian diet? The following food list is divided into three macronutrients that are carbohydrates, protein, and fats.

Food to Eat
Good Carbs:

Vegetables - Leafy greens like kale, spinach, collard, Swiss chards, lettuce, and asparagus. Low-carb vegetables like green beans, broccoli, cauliflower, summer squash, zucchini, garlic, ginger, onion, tomatoes, cucumber, mushrooms, eggplants, bell peppers, olives, avocado.

Herbs - basil, thyme, oregano, rosemary, parsley, and coriander.

Spices – salt, black pepper, red chili powder, cayenne pepper, cumin, cinnamon, nutmeg

Fruits – Berries that are low in sugar that are blueberries, strawberries, raspberries, and strawberries. Lemon and lemon juice.

Low-sugar condiments, dressing, and sauces – soy sauce, hot sauces, tomato ketchup (sugar-free), Worcestershire sauce, organic mayonnaise.

Sugar – Stevia, erythritol, swerve sweetener and any low-carb sweetener.

Good Protein:

Meat alternate – organic tempeh, seitan, tofu.

Nuts – pecan, almond, macadamia, pistachio, cashew, peanut, hazelnut, walnut, pine nut, Brazil nut.

Seeds – Chia seeds, flaxseeds, hemp seeds, pumpkin seeds.

Egg, organic and pastured

Organic dairy products

Miso paste

Hemp protein powder and any low-carb protein powder.

Good Fat:

Cocoa butter, peanut butter, almond butter, grass-fed butter and butter made from any of the above-mentioned nuts.

Healthy oil – olive oil, coconut oil, avocado oil, Flaxseed oil, MCT oil.

Coconut cream and whipping cream, all-full-fat.

Cheese – cream cheese, cottage cheese, parmesan cheese, Swiss cheese, Feta cheese, cheddar cheese, all full-fat.

Coconut milk, full-fat and unsweetened.

Greek yogurt and coconut yogurt, all full-fat.

Food to Avoid

Grains - cereal, wheat, rice, corn and items made from them like bread, pasta, chips, crackers, pretzels.

Legumes and millets – peas, beans, chickpeas, lentils.

Food items made from refined flour and sugar.

Drinks - cold drinks, hot drinks and artificial juices.

Vegetables - starchy veggies, yams, potatoes and sweet potatoes.

Fruits – Apple, banana, orange, pear etc.

Honey and agave syrup.

This list has got you covered with all the pantry items to plan a Ketogenic vegetarian food. Read chapter 5 to get started with the cooking.

Chapter 4: Tips

Here are five steps to get started with keto vegetarian diet:

1- Reducing carb:

   The first goal of a Ketogenic diet is to get into ketosis as soon as possible. For this, reduce carb intake up to 20gm per day. Now in a Ketogenic vegetarian diet, this means cutting off vegetarian high protein sources that are high in carbs like grains, legumes, and millets. Also, make sure to steer away from any low-fat items, fruits, and starchy vegetables. Look in the food list to know how to fill your pantry with the relevant food.

2- Addition of Protein in every meal:

   Animals aren't the only of protein. There are plant-based ingredients that are high in protein and suitable for Keto vegetarian diet. These food items are nuts, seeds. For a Ketogenic diet, the portion of protein is between 1.2 and 1.7 gram per kg of body weight. You can also use eggs, Greek yogurt, hemp seeds, cheeses and butter to get most of the high-quality proteins.

3- Serve Low-carb vegetables twice a day:

   Serve Keto vegetarian-friendly vegetables between 1 to 3 servings twice a day. For this use, vegetables that have a delicious taste with a nice dose of dietary fiber and that should meet your macronutrient needs. Vegetables like spinach, zucchini, avocado, Brussels sprouts, and cauliflowers are great to go.

4- Using healthy oils for cooking:

   Healthy oils are very good at improving the flavors and texture of food. They also help with the absorption of vitamin A, vitamin D, vitamin E and vitamin K. Not only that, they also keep you full and satisfy with the meal and thus, decreasing craving for more food in an untimely manner. For a Keto diet, use vegetable and seed oil and avoid processed oil like sunflower oil, corn oil, and canola oil. Moreover, use these healthy oils to prepared condiments, sauces and salad dressing.

5- Season with herbs and spices:

   Pairing herbs and spices with other ingredients in Keto vegetarian diet make this diet versatile. They are also a source of micronutrient and provide net carbs, the best of both worlds!

Avoiding Nutrient Deficiencies

A vegetarian Ketogenic diet is devoid of vegetarian high protein from legumes, lentils and grains, and other protein sources that are meats and seafood. Therefore, the diet should be managed in such a way to get back protein along with other nutrients like vitamin, iron, calcium, and magnesium. Eat a variety of food made from nutrient-dense ingredients that a Keto vegetarian is most deficient in. You should regularly use the following ingredients to meet this deficiency.

Vegetables – Spinach, kale, broccoli, mushrooms, artichoke, Brussel sprouts.

Fruits – avocado and olives.

Dairy item – Green yogurt and cheeses.

Seeds – Chia, flaxseeds, hemp seeds, pumpkin seeds

Nuts – Almonds, walnuts, cocoa, dark chocolate.

Chapter 5: 30-Day Meal Plan

Day 1

Breakfast

Asparagus and Tomato Frittata

| Servings: 1 Frittata |

| Preparation time: 10 minutes | Cooking time: 20 minutes | Total time: 30 minutes |

Nutrition Value:
Calories: 88.3 Cal, Carbs: 2.7 g, Net Carbs: 2 g, Fat: 5.3 g, Protein: 7.6 g, Fiber: 0.7 g.

Ingredients:

- 8-ounces asparagus, ends trimmed

- 2/3 cup diced cherry tomatoes

- ¼ cup sliced green onion

- 2 teaspoons minced dill, fresh

- 1 teaspoon salt

- ¾ teaspoon ground black pepper

- 3 teaspoons olive oil

- 4-ounces Feta cheese, crumbled

- 6 eggs, slightly beaten

Method:
- Cut asparagus into 1 ½ inch pieces.

- Switch on the broiler and let preheat.

- Place a large pan over medium-high heat, add oil and when heated, add asparagus.

- Let cook for 4 minutes and then add tomatoes and minced dill.

- Continue cooking for 2 minutes and then pour in beaten eggs.

- Season with salt and black pepper and scatter cheese on top.

- Let cook for 10 minutes or until cheese melts completely and eggs are set, covering the pan.

- Uncover pan and transfer to the broiler or until top is nicely browned.

- When done, divide frittata into four portions, then garnish with green onions and serve.

Lunch

Broccoli and Cheese Fritters

| Servings: 16 fritters |
| Preparation time: 15 minutes | Cooking time: 10 minutes | Total time: 25 minutes |

Nutrition Value:
Calories: 103.9 Cal, Carbs: 3.8 g, Net Carbs: 1.9 g, Fat: 8.3 g, Protein: 4.6 g, Fiber: 1.9 g.

Ingredients:

- ¾ cup almond flour
- 4 ounces broccoli, cut into florets
- ¼ cup chopped dill, fresh
- ½ cup flaxseed meal
- 1 ¼ teaspoon salt, divided
- 1 teaspoon ground black pepper, divided
- 2 teaspoons baking powder
- ½ tablespoon lemon juice
- ¼ cup mayonnaise, organic
- 4 ounces mozzarella cheese, grated
- 2 eggs, slightly beaten

Method:
- Place broccoli florets into a food processor and pulse at high speed or until well processed.
- Then transfer this mixture to a bowl, add almond flour, baking powder, 1 teaspoon salt, ¾ teaspoon black pepper, cheese and ¼ cup flaxseed meal and stir until well mixed.
- Pour in eggs and mix until well incorporated.

- Then shape mixture into evenly sized balls and then coat with remaining flaxseed meal.

- Plug in air fryer, turn temperature dial to preheat at 375 degrees F, punch in 5 minutes on the timer pad and let preheat.

- Place prepared balls into greased fryer basket, then insert it into air fryer and punch in 10 minutes.

- Let cook until fritters are nicely brown, shaking halfway through.

- In the meantime, whisk together mayonnaise, dill, remaining salt and black pepper and lemon juice, set aside until required.

- When the timer goes off, carefully remove fritter from air fryer and serve with a prepared mayonnaise dip.

Dinner

Garlic & Chive Cauliflower Mash

| Servings: 2 cups |
| Preparation time: 10 minutes | Cooking time: 15 minutes | Total time: 25 minutes |

Nutrition Value:
Calories: 178 Cal, Carbs: 7.8 g, Net Carbs: 3 g, Fat: 18 g, Protein: 3 g, Fiber: 4.8 g.

Ingredients:

- 4 cups cauliflower florets
- 1 tablespoon chopped chives, fresh
- 1 clove garlic, peeled
- 1/2 teaspoon salt
- 1/8 teaspoon ground black pepper
- 1/2 teaspoon lemon zest
- 1/4 teaspoon lemon juice
- 1 tablespoon water
- 1/3 cup mayonnaise, organic

Method:

- Place cauliflower florets in a large microwave ovenproof bowl and add garlic, salt, black pepper, water, and mayonnaise.
- Stir until mixed and let microwave for 12 to 15 minutes or until very tender.
- When done, puree this mixture using an electric immersion blender until smooth.
- Add remaining ingredients and pulse until combined.
- Serve immediately with favorite salad.

Day 2

- ## Breakfast

Spinach Artichoke Egg Casserole

| Servings: 12 |
| Preparation time: 10 minutes | Cooking time: 35 minutes | Total time: 45 minutes |

Nutrition Value:
Calories: 141 Cal, Carbs: 3.3 g, Net Carbs: 1.8 g, Fat: 8.5 g, Protein: 11.9 g, Fiber: 1.5 g.

Ingredients:

- 14-ounces artichoke hearts
- 10 ounce chopped spinach
- 1/4 cup minced onion
- 1 teaspoon minced garlic
- 1 teaspoon salt
- 1/2 teaspoon crushed red pepper
- 1/2 teaspoon dried thyme
- 1 cup grated white cheddar cheese
- 1/2 cup grated parmesan cheese
- 16 eggs
- 1/2 cup ricotta cheese
- 1/4 cup almond milk, full-fat and unsweetened

Method:
- Set oven to 350 degrees F and let preheat.
- Crack eggs in a bowl and whisk in milk until well combined.
- Separate leaves from artichoke hearts by breaking into small pieces and add to egg mixture.

- If spinach frozen, thaw it, then squeeze out its moisture completely and add to egg mixture.

- Add remaining ingredients except for ricotta cheese and stir until well mixed.

- Take a 9 by 13-inch baking dish, grease with non-stick cooking spray and pour in prepared mixture.

- Top with dollops of ricotta cheese and then place the dish into the oven.

- Let bake for 30 to 35 minutes or until inserted a skewer into the center of casserole comes out clean.

- Serve straightaway.

Lunch

Cheesy Herb Muffins

| Servings: 8 muffins |
| Preparation time: 5 minutes | Cooking time: 25 minutes | Total time: 30 minutes |

Nutrition Value:
Calories: 216 Cal, Carbs: 5 g, Net Carbs: 2 g, Fat: 20 g, Protein: 7 g, Fiber: 3 g.

Ingredients:

- 1 cup almond flour

- 3 tablespoons coconut flour

- 1/2 teaspoon thyme leaves

- 1/4 teaspoon garlic powder

- 3/4 teaspoon salt

- 1 teaspoon erythritol sweetener, granulated

- 2 teaspoons baking powder

- ¼ teaspoon xanthan gum

- 6 tablespoons vegetarian butter

- 1/2 cup grated sharp cheddar cheese

- 2 eggs

- 1/3 cup almond milk, full-fat and unsweetened

Method:
- Set oven to 375 degrees F and let preheat.

- Place butter in a microwave ovenproof bowl and microwave for 30 seconds at high heat setting or until butter melts completely.

- Into melted butter, add remaining ingredients and mix with a fork until incorporated.

- Take an 8 cups muffin tray, grease with cooking spray and then spoon in prepared muffin batter until each cup is 2/3rd full.

- Place muffin tray into the oven and let bake for 22 to 25 minutes or until top is nicely golden brown and inserted a skewer into each muffin comes out clean.

- When done, take out muffins and let cool slightly before serving.

Dinner

Red Coconut Curry

| Servings: 2 |
| Preparation time: 10 minutes | Cooking time: 25 minutes | Total time: 35 minutes |

Nutrition Value:

Calories: 398 Cal, Carbs: 7.9 g, Net Carbs: 5 g, Fat: 40.7 g, Protein: 5.1 g, Fiber: 2.9 g.

Ingredients:

- 1 cup broccoli florets

- ½ cup baby spinach

- 4 tablespoons coconut oil

- ¼ medium-sized white onion, chopped

- 1 teaspoon minced garlic

- 1 teaspoon minced ginger

- 1 tablespoon red curry paste

- 2 teaspoons soy sauce

- 2 teaspoons fish sauce, unsweetened

- ½ cup coconut cream

Method:

- Place a large skillet pan over medium-high heat, add 2 tablespoons oil and when melted, add onion.

- Let cook for 3 to 4 minutes or until onions are caramelized.

- Stir in garlic and let cook for 30 seconds or until nicely browned.

- Lower heat to medium-low, add broccoli florets, stir until well mixed and continue cooking for 2 minutes.

- Move all the ingredients to one side of the pan and add curry paste to the empty side of the pan.

- Let cook for 1 to 2 minutes or until fragrant and then mix this paste with other ingredients in the pan.

- Add spinach and let cook for 2 to 3 minutes or until wilts.

- Pour in coconut cream, mix until combined and then add remaining oil along with remaining ingredients.

- Simmer curry for 5 to 10 minutes or until sauce is reduced to desired thickness.

- Serve when ready.

Day 3

Breakfast

Cauliflower Hash Brown Bowl

| Servings: 1 bowl |
| Preparation time: 15 minutes | Cooking time: 15 minutes | Total time: 30 minutes |

Nutrition Value:
Calories: 115.2 Cal, Carbs: 6.2 g, Net Carbs: 4 g, Fat: 8.3 g, Protein: 7.4 g, Fiber: 2.2 g.

Ingredients:

- 1/2 avocado, pitted

- 1 1/2 cups cauliflower florets, riced

- 4-ounces mushrooms, sliced

- ¼ cup baby spinach

- 1 green onion, chopped

- 1 ½ teaspoons garlic powder

- 2 ½ teaspoons salt

- 2 teaspoon ground black pepper

- 1 tablespoon olive oil

- 1/2 of a lemon

- ¼ cup tomato salsa, fresh

- 2 eggs

Method:
- Scoop out the flesh of avocado and place into a bowl along with ½ teaspoon garlic powder, ½ teaspoon salt, ½ teaspoon black pepper and lemon juice.

- Mash all the ingredients with a fork until well combined, set aside until required.

- Crack eggs in another bowl, add ½ teaspoon each of salt and black pepper and whisk until frothy.

- Place a large skillet over medium heat, add ½ tablespoon oil and when heated, add mushrooms.

- Let cook for 5 to 7 minutes or until tender and then season with ½ teaspoon each of garlic powder, and salt and black pepper.

- Continue cooking until mushrooms are nicely golden brown and then transfer mushrooms to a plate.

- Switch heat to medium-high, add remaining oil and when heated, add cauliflower rice.

- Season with remaining garlic powder, salt, and black pepper and let cook for 5 minutes or until tender-crisp.

- When done, transfer cauliflower to a separate bowl.

- Switch heat to medium level, return mushrooms to skillet and add spinach and onions.

- Let cook for 1 minute or until leaves wilts.

- Then pour in eggs and let cook until eggs are scrambled to desired consistency.

- Top this mixture over cauliflower and then top with avocado mixture.

- Top with salsa and serve.

Lunch

Greek Salad

| Servings: 4 |
| Preparation time: 10 minutes | Cooking time: 0 minutes | Total time: 10 minutes |

Nutrition Value:
Calories: 118 Cal, Carbs: 7 g, Net Carbs: 5.6 g, Fat: 9 g, Protein: 5.1 g, Fiber: 1.4 g.

Ingredients:

- 2 medium-sized cucumbers
- 16 fluid ounce cherry tomatoes
- 6 black olives
- Half of a small red onion, peeled and diced
- 2 tablespoons fresh dill
- 2 tablespoons olive oil
- 4-ounce feta cheese, cubed

Method:
- Peel cucumbers, then chop and place in a large bowl.
- Cut each cherry tomato into half and add to cucumber.
- Add dill and cheese and toss until just mix.
- Drizzle with olive oil and serve immediately.

Dinner

Gnocchi

| Servings: 5 |
| Preparation time: 25 minutes | Cooking time: 20 minutes | Total time: 45 minutes |

Nutrition Value:
Calories: 243 Cal, Carbs: 8.9 g, Net Carbs: 4.8 g, Fat: 13.8 g, Protein: 19.6 g, Fiber: 4.1 g.

Ingredients:

- 2 cups almond flour

- 1 teaspoon lemon zest

- 1 teaspoon thyme leaves

- 1 teaspoon salt

- ½ teaspoon ground black pepper

- 1/2 cup vegetarian butter

- 1 egg

- 1 egg yolk

- 2 cups shredded full-fat mozzarella cheese

Method:
- Place cheese in a microwave ovenproof bowl, add ¼ cup butter and let microwave for 1 minute at high-speed setting.

- Then stir the mixture and continue microwave for another minute.

- Stir again until well combined and let cool for 2 minutes.

- Whisk in egg and egg yolk until combined and then gradually stir in flour using a spoon until incorporated and soft dough comes together.

- Transfer dough to a clean working space and knead for 5 minutes.

- Knead in 1 to 2 tablespoon flours if the dough is too wet or knead in 1 to 2 tablespoon waters if the dough is too dry.

- Shape dough into 1-inch diameter roll and then cut into ½ inch wide pieces.

- Place these gnocchi pieces on a baking tray and let freeze for 10 minutes in a freezer or until firm.

- When ready to cook, fill a large pot half full of water and stir in 1 tablespoon salt.

- Bring the water to a gentle boil and add the gnocchi in a small batch.

- Let boil for 2 minutes or until gnocchi starts to float and then remove to a plate lined with paper towel.

- Boil remaining gnocchi in the same manner and let cool for 5 minutes.

- Prepare sauce for gnocchi by place a large pan over medium heat, add remaining butter and when melt, add thyme and lemon zest.

- Let cool for 2 minutes or until fragrant.

- Add boiled gnocchi to the pan, toss to coat and let cook for 2 minutes or until heated through.

- Season with salt and black pepper and serve.

Breakfast

Cheesy Thyme Waffles

| Servings: 4 waffles |
| Preparation time: 10 minutes | Cooking time: 25 minutes | Total time: 35 minutes |

Nutrition Value:
Calories: 203.2 Cal, Carbs: 9.2 g, Net Carbs: 5.8 g, Fat: 15.9 g, Protein: 15 g, Fiber: 3.4 g.

Ingredients:

- ½ large head of cauliflower, cut into florets
- 2 stalks of green onion, sliced
- 1 cup collard greens
- 1 teaspoon garlic powder
- ½ teaspoon salt
- 1 tablespoon sesame seed
- ½ teaspoon ground black pepper
- 2 teaspoons chopped thyme
- 1 tablespoon olive oil
- 1 cup grated mozzarella cheese
- 1/3 cup grated Parmesan cheese
- 2 eggs

Method:
- Place cauliflower florets in a food processor and process for 2 minutes at high speed or until mixture resembles rice.
- Add onion, collard greens and thyme and pulse for another minute or until well combined.

- Transfer the mixture to a large bowl and add remaining ingredients.

- Stir until well mixed.

- Switch on the waffle iron, grease with non-stick cooking spray and when preheated, spoon the prepared waffle mixture in it.

- Cook for 2 cycles or until steam rises from the waffle iron and then transfer waffle to a serving plate.

- Cook remaining waffles in the same manner and serve.

Lunch

Mushroom Risotto

| Servings: 6 |
| Preparation time: 20 minutes | Cooking time: 30 minutes | Total time: 50 minutes |

Nutrition Value:
Calories: 143.75 Cal, Carbs: 9.31 g, Net Carbs: 7.5 g, Fat: 11.3 g, Protein: 5.25 g, Fiber: 3 g.

Ingredients:

- 5 cups cauliflower florets, riced
- 8 ounces cremini mushrooms, sliced
- 1 large shallot, minced
- 1 small white onion, peeled and diced
- 2 tablespoons chopped parsley
- 4 teaspoons minced garlic
- 1 teaspoon sea salt
- ¾ teaspoon ground black pepper
- 2 tablespoons vegetarian butter
- 2 tablespoons olive oil
- 1/2 cup grated Parmesan cheese
- 1 cup heavy cream, full-fat
- 2 cup vegetable stock, divided

Method:

- Place a large pan over medium heat, add butter and olive oil and when heated, add onion, shallot, and garlic.
- Let cook for 5 minutes or until onions are softened.

- Add mushrooms to pan, pour in 1 cup stock and continue cooking for 5 minutes or until mushrooms are tender.

- Add cauliflower rice along with remaining stock and let cook for 10 minutes, stirring frequently.

- Then switch heat to low and stir in remaining ingredients to the pan.

- Let simmer for 10 to 15 minutes or until risotto is slightly thick/

- Serve immediately.

Dinner

Mac & Cheese

| Servings: 6 |
| Preparation time: 15 minutes | Cooking time: 2 hours | Total time: 35 minutes |

Nutrition Value:
Calories: 340.8 Cal, Carbs: 6.4 g, Net Carbs: 4 g, Fat: 29.9 g, Protein: 12.7 g, Fiber: 2.4 g.

Ingredients:

- 1 large head of cauliflower, cut into florets
- 1/4 cup diced pickled jalapeno
- 1/2 teaspoon onion powder
- 1/2 teaspoon garlic powder
- 1 tablespoon salt
- 1/4 teaspoon paprika, organic
- 1/2 teaspoon yellow mustard
- 1/2 stick of vegetarian butter
- 4 ounces cream cheese, full-fat
- 8 ounces grated cheddar cheese
- 2/3 cup half and half cream

Method:

- Fill a large pot half full of water, add salt and bring to boil.
- Then add cauliflower florets and let cook for 5 minutes.
- Then drain cauliflower florets and return them to pot.
- Add remaining ingredients except for paprika, stir until well combined and then spoon the mixture into a 6-quart slow cooker.

- Cover slow cooker with its lid, plug in and let cook for 2 to 2 ½ hours at high heat setting or until cooked through.

- When done, transfer mac and cheese to a serving platter, let cool slightly, then sprinkle with paprika and serve.

Day 5

Breakfast

Brownie Muffins

| Servings: 6 brownies |
| Preparation time: 10 minutes | Cooking time: 25 minutes | Total time: 35 minutes |

Nutrition Value:
Calories: 193 Cal, Carbs: 11.5 g, Net Carbs: 4.37 g, Fat: 14.1 g, Protein: 7 g, Fiber: 7.18 g.

Ingredients:

- 1 cup flaxseed meal

- ¼ cup slivered almonds

- ¼ cup cocoa powder, unsweetened

- ½ teaspoon salt

- 1 tablespoon ground cinnamon

- ½ tablespoon baking powder

- 1 teaspoon vanilla extract, unsweetened

- 1 teaspoon apple cider vinegar, organic

- ¼ cup caramel syrup

- 2 tablespoons coconut oil

- 1 egg

- ½ cup pumpkin puree

Method:
- Set oven to 350 degrees F and let preheat.
- Place flaxseed meal in a bowl along with cocoa powder, cinnamon, baking powder and salt, and stir until mixed.

- Place remaining ingredients except for almonds into another bowl and whisk until mixed.

- Gradually stir in flaxseed meal mixture until incorporated.

- Take a 6 cups muffin tray, line with muffin cups and then fill with prepared brownie mixture until each cup is 2/3rd full.

- Sprinkle with almonds and let bake for 15 minutes or until brownies are risen slightly and inserted a skewer into brownies come out clean.

- When done, take out muffin cups from muffin tray and let cool slightly before serving.

Lunch

Roasted Caprese Tomatoes Salad

| Servings: 4 |
| Preparation time: 10 minutes | Cooking time: 30 minutes | Total time: 40 minutes |

Nutrition Value:
Calories: 190.7 Cal, Carbs: 8.4 g, Net Carbs: 4.6 g, Fat: 13.5 g, Protein: 7.8 g, Fiber: 3.8 g.

Ingredients:

- 4 large tomatoes, halved
- 4 leaves of basil
- 1 teaspoon salt
- 1 teaspoon ground black pepper
- 4 thin slices of Mozzarella cheese
- 1 tablespoon olive oil
- 2 tablespoons apple cider vinegar, organic
- 6-ounce wild rockets

For the dressing

- ¼ cup basil leaves
- 1 clove of garlic
- ½ teaspoon salt
- 2 tablespoons olive oil

Method:
- Set oven to 350 degrees F and let preheat.
- Arrange halved tomatoes, cut-side up, on to a baking sheet, then drizzle with vinegar and oil and season with salt and black pepper.

- Place the baking sheet into the oven and let bake for 20 to 25 minutes or until roasted.

- In the meantime, place all the ingredients for dressing in a food processor and pulse until smooth, set aside until required.

- Then top each tomato half with a mozzarella cheese stick and continue roasting for another 5 minutes.

- Then place a basil leaf onto the bottom half of half tomato and cover with its top half.

- Spread wild rocket onto a serving platter, top with tomatoes, and then drizzle with prepared dressing and serve.

Dinner

Cauliflower Fried Rice

| Servings: 4 |
| Preparation time: 10 minutes | Cooking time: 10 minutes | Total time: 20 minutes |

Nutrition Value:
Calories: 114 Cal, Carbs: 6 g, Net Carbs: 5 g, Fat: 8 g, Protein: 4 g, Fiber: 1 g.

Ingredients:

- 12 ounces riced cauliflower
- 1/4 cup carrot, diced
- 2 large green onions, green and white parts cut separately
- 2 teaspoons minced garlic
- 2 tablespoons soy sauce
- 2 tablespoons olive oil
- 1 teaspoon toasted sesame oil
- 1 egg, slightly beaten

Method:

- Place a large skillet over medium-high heat, add oil and when heated, add cauliflower rice and carrots.
- Let cook for 5 minutes or until softened.
- Add white parts of green onion and continue cooking for 3 minutes.
- Then stir in garlic and let cook for 1 minute.
- Pour in beaten eggs and stir until well mixed.
- Let cook for 2 minutes or until eggs are scrambled, stirring frequently.
- Stir in sesame oil and soy sauce and taste to adjust seasoning.
- Serve straightaway.

Day 6

Breakfast

Porridge

| Servings: 1 |
| Preparation time: 10 minutes | Cooking time: 10 minutes | Total time: 20 minutes |

Nutrition Value:
Calories: 249 Cal, Carbs: 19.7 g, Net Carbs: 5.78 g, Fat: 13.1 g, Protein: 17.8 g, Fiber: 14 g.

Ingredients:

- 2 tablespoons coconut flour

- 3 tablespoons flaxseed meal

- 1 tablespoon chopped almonds

- ½ tablespoon erythritol, powdered

- 2 tablespoons vegan protein powder, any flavor

- 1 ½ cups almond milk, full-fat and unsweetened

- Sliced fruit for serving

Method:
- Place flour in a bowl, add flaxseed meal along with protein powder and stir until mixed.

- Place a saucepan over medium heat, add flaxseed mixture, then pour in milk and let cook for 10 minutes or until thickened to desired consistency.

- Stir in sweetener and transfer to a serving bowl.

- Top with almond and fruit slices and serve.

Lunch

Zucchini Noodle Egg Drop Soup

| Servings: 6 |
| Preparation time: 15 minutes | Cooking time: 20 minutes | Total time: 35 minutes |

Nutrition Value:
Calories: 195.1 Cal, Carbs: 20.4 g, Net Carbs: 12.3 g, Fat: 23.5 g, Protein: 11.5 g, Fiber: 8.1 g.

Ingredients:

- 4 medium-sized zucchinis
- 2 cups sliced scallions, divided
- 5 cups shiitake mushrooms, sliced
- 2 tablespoons grated ginger
- 1 ½ teaspoon salt
- ¾ teaspoon ground black pepper
- ½ teaspoons red pepper flakes
- 3 tablespoons cornstarch
- 5 tablespoons soy sauce
- 2 tablespoons olive oil
- 8 cups vegetable stock, divided
- 2 cups and 1 tablespoon water, divided
- 4 eggs, slightly beaten

Method:
- Rinse zucchini and then spiralized into thin noodles using noodle blade with spiralizer, set aside until required.

- Place a large pot over medium-high heat, add oil and when heated, add ginger and let cook for 2 minutes or until fragrant.

- Add mushroom along with 1 tablespoon water and let cook for 3 to 5 minutes or until mushrooms start losing their moisture.

- Pour in remaining water along with 7 cups vegetable stock, stir in 1 ½ cups scallions, red pepper flakes and soy sauce and bring the mixture to boil.

- In the meantime, stir in cornstarch into remaining 1 cup of stock and then add to boiling soup.

- Let cook for 5 minutes or until soup starts to thicken.

- Stir in salt and black pepper along with zucchini noodles and let cook for 2 minutes or until noodles are tender-crisp.

- Garnish with scallions and ladle soup into bowls to serve.

Dinner

Mexican Cauliflower Patties

| Servings: 8 patties |
| Preparation time: 10 minutes | Cooking time: 40 minutes | Total time: 50 minutes |

Nutrition Value:
Calories: 266 Cal, Carbs: 7 g, Net Carbs: 6 g, Fat: 22 g, Protein: 15 g, Fiber: 1 g.

Ingredients:

- ¼ cup almond flour

- 1 small head of cauliflower, cut into florets

- 3 scallions, minced

- ¼ cup chopped cilantro

- 1/4 teaspoon salt

- 1 tablespoon Mexican spice mix

- 2 eggs, slightly beaten

- 1 cup grated sharp cheddar cheese

- 2 tablespoons coconut oil

- 2 wedges of lime

Method:
- Set oven to 300 degrees F and let preheat.

- In the meantime, place a large pot half full of water, fit it with a steamer basket and bring water to boil.

- When the water starts boiling, add florets to steamer basket, then cover pot and let cook for 7 to 8 minutes or until florets are tender.

- Meanwhile, place flour in a bowl and add scallion, cilantro, salt, spice mix, and egg.

- Stir until well combined and set aside until required.

- When cauliflower florets cooking time is over, remove steamer basket from the pot and let cool for 10 minutes.

- Then puree cauliflower florets using electric stand mixer until smooth and then add the egg mixture in it.

- Stir until well mixed and then stir in cheese.

- Place a large pan over medium heat, add 1 tablespoon oil and when heated, add ¼ cup of cauliflower mixture in four portions.

- Cover pan with a lid and let cook for 5 to 7 minutes per side or until nicely browned and cooked through.

- Cook remaining patties in the same manner and serve with lime wedges.

Day 7

Breakfast

Zucchini Bagels

| Servings: 4 bagels |
| Preparation time: 15 minutes | Cooking time: 20 minutes | Total time: 35 minutes |

Nutrition Value:
Calories: 176 Cal, Carbs: 14 g, Net Carbs: 7 g, Fat: 18.8 g, Protein: 15 g, Fiber: 7 g.

Ingredients:

- 3 medium-sized Zucchini, grated

- 1/3 cup coconut flour

- 1/4 teaspoon sea salt

- 1 teaspoon baking powder

- 1 cup grated Mozzarella cheese

- 2 egg

Method:

- Set oven to 400 degrees F and let preheat.

- In the meantime, place grated zucchini into a colander, sprinkle with sea salt, mix and let sit for 20 moistures to an hour.

- Then drain zucchini, place into a cheesecloth and wrap it.

- Squeeze cloth tightly to drain moisture from zucchini completely and place dry cauliflower in a bowl.

- Add remaining ingredients except for cheese and stir until combined.

- Place cheese in a microwave proof bowl and microwave for 1 minute and 30 seconds or until melt completely.

- Immediately add mozzarella to flour mixture and knead until smooth dough comes together.

- Take a bagel mold, grease with non-stick cooking spray and press prepared the dough in its cavity.

- Prepare remaining dough into three more greased bagel molds.

- Place bagel molds onto a baking sheet and then place into the oven to bake for 15 to 20 minutes or until nicely golden.

- When done, take out bagels and serve as per liking.

Lunch

Cauliflower Crust Grilled Cheese Sandwich

| Servings: 2 |
| Preparation time: 10 minutes | Cooking time: 40 minutes | Total time: 50 minutes |

Nutrition Value:
Calories: 496.6 Cal, Carbs: 20.7 g, Net Carbs: 13.2 g, Fat: 30.1 g, Protein: 39.7 g, Fiber: 7.5 g.

Ingredients:

- 3 cups riced cauliflower
- ½ teaspoon sea salt
- ¼ teaspoon ground black pepper
- 1 tablespoon vegetarian butter
- 1/3 cup grated sharp cheddar cheese
- ½ cup grated mozzarella cheese
- 1 egg

Method:

- Place a baking rack into middle shelf of the oven, then set the temperature to 450 degrees F and let preheat.
- Place riced cauliflower into a microwave proof bowl and microwave for 8 minutes at high heat setting or until cooked through.
- Transfer riced cauliflower to a cheesecloth, wrap it and then squeeze tightly to drain moisture completely.
- Transfer this dry riced cauliflower, add salt, black pepper, mozzarella cheese, and egg.
- Stir until well combined and then spread this mixture onto a baking sheet, lined with parchment paper.

- Shape mixture into four squares of equal size and then bake for 16 minutes or until nicely golden.

- When done, remove baking sheet from oven and let cool for 10 minutes.

- Then place a pan over medium heat and let heat.

- Butter one side of each cauliflower slice with butter and place into the pan, buttered side up.

- Sprinkle with cheddar cheese and top with another slice, buttered side up.

- Let cook for 2 to 4 minutes, then flip and continue cooking for 2 to 4 minutes.

- Cook remaining sandwich in the same manner and serve.

Dinner

Boiled Egg Curry

| Servings: 4 |
| Preparation time: 10 minutes | Cooking time: 30 minutes | Total time: 40 minutes |

Nutrition Value:
Calories: 511 Cal, Carbs: 11 g, Net Carbs: 6 g, Fat: 46 g, Protein: 17 g, Fiber: 5 g.

Ingredients:

- 1 Serrano chili pepper, chopped

- 2 cups green beans, trimmed and diced

- 1 tablespoon chopped cilantro

- 1 small white onion, peeled and diced

- 1 tablespoon minced garlic

- 1/2 teaspoon grated ginger

- 3 tablespoons olive oil

- 1 teaspoon salt

- 1/2 teaspoon ground black pepper

- 1 teaspoon turmeric powder

- 1/2 teaspoon ground coriander

- 1/2 teaspoon ground cumin

- 1 teaspoon garam masala

- 1 tablespoon flaked almonds

- 1/4 cup tomato puree

- 14 ounces coconut cream

- 8 eggs, boiled and shelled

Method:

- Place a medium saucepan over medium heat, add 2 tablespoons oil and when heated, add onion, chili pepper, and garlic.

- Let cook for 3 to 5 minutes, then switch heat to a low level and stir in ginger, salt, black pepper, turmeric powder, ground coriander and cumin, garam masala and tomato puree.

- Let cook for 2 minutes and then stir in coconut cream and let simmer for 10 minutes.

- In the meantime, place a frying pan over medium heat, add remaining oil and when heated, add peeled boiled eggs.

- Let fry them until all sides are nicely brown and crispy.

- When the sauce is ready, add crispy eggs along with green beans.

- Let simmer for 5 to 8 minutes.

- Garnish with cilantro and almonds and serve.

Day 8

Breakfast

Eggs in Avocado

| Servings: 2 |
| Preparation time: 10 minutes | Cooking time: 25 minutes | Total time: 35 minutes |

Nutrition Value:
Calories: 215 Cal, Carbs: 8 g, Net Carbs: 5.4 g, Fat: 18.1 g, Protein: 9.1 g, Fiber: 2.6 g.

Ingredients:

- 1 large avocado, halved and pitted

- ¾ teaspoon salt

- ¾ teaspoon ground black pepper

- Thyme for garnishing

- 2 eggs

- 1 teaspoon coconut oil

Method:
- Cut off a small part from the bottom of each avocado half to make it sit straight and then using a spoon, scoop out enough flesh to fill an egg.

- Crack an egg and place its egg yolk and egg white in two small bowls.

- Crack another egg and add its egg white to previous egg white and egg yolk to another bowl.

- Add salt and black pepper to egg white and whisk until combined.

- Place a skillet pan over medium-high heat, add oil and when heat, add avocado halves, cut side down, and let sear for 30 seconds or until nicely golden brown.

- Turn heat to low, then flip avocado halves, pour egg whites into avocado cavities and cover the pan with a lid.

- Let cook for 15 to 20 minutes or until egg whites are almost set and then top egg white with egg yolk.

- Cover pan and continue cooking for 3 to 5 minutes or until egg yolks are cooked to the desired level.

- Transfer avocado halves to the serving plate, sprinkle with thyme and serve.

Lunch

Moroccan Roasted Green Beans

| Servings: 6 |
| Preparation time: 10 minutes | Cooking time: 30 minutes | Total time: 40 minutes |

Nutrition Value:
Calories: 50.7 Cal, Carbs: 5.3 g, Net Carbs: 2.1 g, Fat: 2.8 g, Protein: 1.1 g, Fiber: 3.2 g.

Ingredients:

- 6 cups green beans, trimmed
- 1 teaspoon salt
- 1/2 teaspoon ground black pepper
- 1 tablespoon Ras el Hanout seasoning
- 2 tablespoons olive oil

Method:
- Set oven to 400 degrees F and let preheat.
- Place green beans on a large cookie sheet, drizzle with olive oil and sprinkle with salt, black pepper, and seasoning.
- Place cookie sheet into the heated oven and let cook for 20 minutes or until roasted.
- Then remove cookie sheet from the oven, stir beans and continue roasting for another 10 minutes.
- Serve warm.

Dinner

Curried Cauliflower Rice Kale Soup

| Servings: 4 |

| Preparation time: 10 minutes | Cooking time: 25 minutes | Total time: 35 minutes |

Nutrition Value:

Calories: 162 Cal, Carbs: 20.6 g, Net Carbs: 11.8 g, Fat: 8.6 g, Protein: 6.2 g, Fiber: 8.8 g.

Ingredients:

- 4 cups riced cauliflower

- 8 kale leaves, stemmed trimmed and leaves chopped

- 2 cups chopped carrots

- 3/4 cup red onion, peeled and chopped

- 1 teaspoon garlic powder

- 1 teaspoon minced garlic

- 1 ½ teaspoon salt

- 1/4 teaspoon sea salt

- 1/2 teaspoon ground black pepper

- 1/2 teaspoon red pepper flakes

- 1/2 teaspoon paprika, organic

- 1/2 teaspoon cumin powder

- 3 tablespoons curry powder

- 5 tablespoons olive oil, divided

- 4 cups vegetable stock

- 1 cup coconut milk, full-fat

Method:

- Set oven to 400 degrees F and let preheat.

- Place riced cauliflower in a bowl, add garlic powder, salt, paprika, cumin, curry powder and 3 tablespoons oil.

- Stir until well mixed and spoon this mixture in a baking dish.

- Spread this mixture evenly into baking dish and then place into the oven to bake for 20 to 22 minutes or until tender and slightly undercooked.

- When done, remove baking dish, stir and set aside until cooled.

- Then a large pot over medium heat, add remaining oil along with minced garlic and let cook for 5 minutes or until sauté.

- Add kale, carrots and onion, roasted riced cauliflower, black pepper, sea salt, red chili pepper, and pour in vegetable stock and coconut milk.

- Bring the soup to boil and let simmer for 20 minutes or until vegetables are cooked through.

- When done, ladle soup into bowls and serve.

Day 9

Breakfast

Macro Cakes

| Servings: 20 pancakes |
| Preparation time: 10 minutes | Cooking time: 20 minutes | Total time: 30 minutes |

Nutrition Value:
Calories: 100 Cal, Carbs: 1 g, Net Carbs: 1 g, Fat: 8 g, Protein: 6 g, Fiber: 0 g.

Ingredients:

- 2-ounce protein powder

- 1 teaspoon vanilla extract, unsweetened

- 4 tablespoons vegetarian butter

- 8-ounce cream cheese, softened

- 8 eggs

- Berries for serving

Method:
- Crack eggs in a bowl, add cream cheese and butter and whisk using an electric hand immersion blender until well combined.

- Whisk in protein powder until mixed well.

- Place a skillet pan over medium heat and when heated, add a spoonful of pancake mixture in portions until pan is filled.

- Let cook for 2 minutes per side and then transfer to a plate.

- Use remaining batter to cook pancakes in the same manner and serve with berries.

Lunch

Falafel with Tahini Sauce

| Servings: 4 |
| Preparation time: 10 minutes | Cooking time: 20 minutes | Total time: 30 minutes |

Nutrition Value:
Calories: 281 Cal, Carbs: 9 g, Net Carbs: 5 g, Fat: 24 g, Protein: 8 g, Fiber: 4 g.

Ingredients:

- 1 cup cauliflower florets, pureed
- 3 tablespoons coconut flour
- 1/2 cup slivered almonds, ground
- 2 tablespoons parsley, chopped
- 1 teaspoon minced garlic
- 1 teaspoon salt
- 1/2 teaspoon cayenne pepper
- 1 tablespoon ground cumin
- 1/2 tablespoon ground coriander
- 2 tablespoons olive oil
- 2 eggs

Tahini Sauce:

- 2 tablespoons tahini paste
- 1 teaspoon minced garlic
- 1/2 teaspoon salt
- 1 tablespoon lemon juice
- 3 tablespoons water

Method:

- Place pureed cauliflower and almonds in a bowl along with remaining ingredients for falafels.

- Stir until well combined and then shape mixture into 8 patties, each about 3-inch thick.

- Place a pan over medium heat, add oil and when heated, add four patties.

- Let cook for 4 to 5 minutes per side or until nicely browned and then transfer to a plate lined with paper towels.

- Cook remaining patties in the same manner.

- In the meantime, prepare tahini sauce by whisking together all the ingredients for the sauce.

- Garnish falafels with parsley and serve with tahini sauce.

Dinner

Broccoli Cheese Soup

| Servings: 4 |
| Preparation time: 10 minutes | Cooking time: 15 minutes | Total time: 25 minutes |

Nutrition Value:
Calories: 544 Cal, Carbs: 10.5 g, Net Carbs: 8.2 g, Fat: 46.7 g, Protein: 21 g, Fiber: 2.2 g.

Ingredients:

- 1 large head of broccoli, cut into florets
- 1 cup diced white onion
- 1 teaspoon sea salt
- 1/2 teaspoon ground black pepper
- 2 cups grated cheddar cheese
- 1 cup heavy whipping cream
- 4 cups vegetable stock

Method:

- Plug in instant pot and add broccoli florets along with onion, salt, black pepper, and cheese.
- Pour in the stock, stir until mixed and then close the instant pot with its lid.
- Press the soup button, adjust cooking time to 7 minutes and let cook at high pressure.
- When the timer beep, press cancel and do quick pressure release.
- Transfer 1 cup of this soup to a bowl, add cream and then pulse using an electric immersion hand blender until smooth.
- Stir this mixture into soup, then press sauté button and let the soup simmer for 5 minutes or until slightly thick.
- Taste to adjust seasoning and serve.

Breakfast

Salted Chocolate Chip Cookies

| Servings: 18 cookies |
| Preparation time: 15 minutes | Cooking time: 12 minutes | Total time: 27 minutes |

Nutrition Value:
Calories: 149 Cal, Carbs: 3 g, Net Carbs: 2.5 g, Fat: 13 g, Protein: 2.2 g, Fiber: 1.5 g.

Ingredients:

- 4.2-ounces almond flour

- 2 tablespoons coconut flour

- 4-ounce dark chocolate bar, chopped

- 2.5-ounce pecans, grounded

- 1/2 teaspoon xanthan gum

- 1 teaspoon salt

- 7 tablespoons erythritol

- 1/2 teaspoon baking soda

- 1 teaspoon vanilla extract, unsweetened

- 6-ounce vegetarian butter

- 1 egg

- Sea salt to garnish

Method:
- Place flours in a medium bowl along with xanthan gum, salt, and baking powder and whisk until combined.

- Place butter in another bowl and using an electric immersion blender, pulse butter at high speed until creamy for 1 to 2 minutes.

- Add erythritol and continue creaming for 8 minutes or until fluffy.

- Add eggs and vanilla and blend until incorporated.

- Gradually blend in flour mixture at low speed and then fold in chocolate and pecan pieces.

- Cover bowl with plastic wrap and let chill in the refrigerator for 1 hour.

- Set oven to 350 degrees F and let preheat until cookies are ready to bake.

- After 1 hour of chilling time, transfer cookie dough to a clean working space, divide into 18 rounds, each of 3 1/2-inch cookies.

- Flatten each round using a rolling pin and place on cookie sheets.

- Place cookie sheet into the oven to bake for 10 to 12 minutes or until nicely golden brown, turning cookie sheet halfway through.

- When done, sprinkle sea salt over cookies and let cool completely on wire racks before serving.

Lunch

Spinach Stuffed Mushrooms

| Servings: 8 |
| Preparation time: 10 minutes | Cooking time: 28 minutes | Total time: 38 minutes |

Nutrition Value:
Calories: 255 Cal, Carbs: 8.4 g, Net Carbs: 4.9 g, Fat: 18.5 g, Protein: 16.6 g, Fiber: 3.5 g.

Ingredients:

- 4 medium-sized Portobello mushrooms, cored
- 10-ounces frozen spinach, thawed, drained and cooked
- 14-ounces artichoke hearts, drained and chopped
- 2 teaspoons minced garlic
- 1 teaspoon salt
- ¾ teaspoon ground black pepper
- 2 tablespoons olive oil
- 4 ounces cream cheese, softened
- 1/2 cup grated Parmesan cheese
- 2 tablespoons sour cream, organic and full-fat
- 3 ounces grated Mozzarella cheese

Method:
- Remove stems and gills in mushrooms, then crush with olive oil and place on a baking pan.
- Switch on broiler, place baking pan in the middle shelf of broiler and let cook for 5 minutes per side or until tender.
- Set oven to 375 degrees F and let preheat.

- In the meantime, squeeze moisture from spinach completely, add to a bowl and add remaining ingredient except for Mozzarella cheese.

- Stir until well combined and then spoon this mixture into broiled mushrooms.

- Top with Mozzarella cheese and let bake for 12 to 15 minutes or until cheese melts.

- Then turn on broiler and let broil for 3 minutes or until top is nicely browned.

- Serve straightaway.

Dinner

Greens & Spinach Soup

| Servings: 6 |
| Preparation time: 15 minutes | Cooking time: 30 minutes | Total time: 45 minutes |

Nutrition Value:
Calories: 143 Cal, Carbs: 13 g, Net Carbs: 9 g, Fat: 11 g, Protein: 7 g, Fiber: 4 g.

Ingredients:

- 5 cups chopped mustard greens, fresh
- 1 cup chopped white onions
- 1 tablespoon chopped jalapeño
- 5 cups chopped spinach, fresh
- 1 tablespoon grated ginger
- 1 tablespoon minced garlic
- 3/4 teaspoon salt
- 1/2 teaspoon paprika, organic
- 1 teaspoon coriander seeds
- 1/2 teaspoon turmeric powder
- 1 teaspoon cumin seeds
- 3 tablespoons olive oil, divided
- 1/2 teaspoon fenugreek seeds
- 3 cups coconut milk, full-fat

Method:
- Place a large pot over medium heat, add 1 tablespoon oil and when heated, add seeds of cumin, coriander, and fenugreek.

- Let cook for 2 to 3 minutes or until nicely browned and fragrant.

- Add onion and let cook for 5 minutes or until golden brown.

- Add jalapeño, ½ teaspoon garlic, and ginger and let cook for 2 to 3 minutes or until pepper is softened.

- Add spinach and green and continue cooking for 7 to 10 minutes or until spinach leaves wilt.

- Season with salt, then pour in milk and remove the pot from heat.

- Blend soup using an electric hand immersion blender at high speed for 3 to 5 minutes until creamy and smooth.

- Return pot over medium heat and bring to simmer for 2 minutes.

- Then transfer soup into serving bowl.

- In the meantime, place a small saucepan over medium heat, add remaining oil and when heated, add remaining garlic and let cook for 2 minutes or until golden and fragrant.

- Stir in paprika and drizzle over soup.

- Stir soup and serve.

Day 11

Breakfast

Cheesy Cauliflower Bread

| Servings: 1 Bread |
| Preparation time: 10 minutes | Cooking time: 35 minutes | Total time: 45 minutes |

Nutrition Value:
Calories: 66.7 Cal, Carbs: 4.2 g, Net Carbs: 2.2 g, Fat: 3.3 g, Protein: 6.4g, Fiber: 2 g.

Ingredients:

- 1 large head of cauliflower, riced

- 2 teaspoons chopped parsley

- 1 ½ tablespoons minced garlic

- 1 teaspoon salt

- ½ teaspoon ground black pepper

- 1/2 teaspoon dried oregano

- ¼ teaspoon crushed red pepper flakes

- 2 eggs

- 3 cup shredded mozzarella cheese, divided

- 1/2 cup grated parmesan cheese

Method:
- Set oven to 425 degrees F and let preheat.

- Place riced cauliflower in a bowl, add garlic, salt, black pepper, oregano, 1 cup mozzarella cheese and parmesan cheese.

- Stir until well combined and a smooth dough comes together.

- Take a baking sheet, line with parchment sheet, then place dough in it and pat into an evenly thick crust.

- Place crust into the oven and let bake for 25 minutes or until nicely golden brown.

- When done, remove baking sheet from the oven, sprinkle with red pepper flakes, parsley, and remaining mozzarella cheese.

- Return crust into the oven and let bake for 5 to 10 minutes or until cheese melts.

- Slice to serve.

Lunch

Rutabaga Fritters with Avocado

| Servings: 4 |
| Preparation time: 20 minutes | Cooking time: 15 minutes | Total time: 35 minutes |

Nutrition Value:
Calories: 441 Cal, Carbs: 11.4 g, Net Carbs: 5.5 g, Fat: 40 g, Protein: 8.4 g, Fiber: 5.9 g.

Ingredients:

- 15-ounce rutabaga, peeled
- 4 avocados
- 5 1/3-ounce leafy greens
- 3 tablespoons coconut flour
- 1 teaspoon salt
- ¼ teaspoon ground black pepper
- 1/8 teaspoon turmeric powder
- 4 tablespoons olive oil
- 8-ounce Halloumi cheese, grated
- 4 eggs

Ranch Mayonnaise

- 1 cup mayonnaise, organic
- 1 tablespoon ranch seasoning

Method:
- Rinse peeled rutabaga and then process it in a food processor and place in a bowl.
- Add cheese along with other ingredients except for avocado, greens, and oil, then stir until well combined and let sit for 5 minutes.

- Shape mixture into 12 patties.

- Place a large frying pan over medium-high heat, add oil and when heated, add patties in a single layer.

- Let cook for 3 to 5 minutes per sides and then transfer to a plate lined with paper towels.

- In the meantime, whisk together ingredients for ranch mayonnaise and set aside.

- Cook remaining patties in the same manner and serve with avocado slices and green and ranch mayonnaise.

Dinner

Spaghetti Squash Casserole

| Servings: 8 |
| Preparation time: 20 minutes | Cooking time: 1 hour and 5 minutes | Total time: 1 hour and 25 minutes |

Nutrition Value:
Calories: 219 Cal, Carbs: 11 g, Net Carbs: 9 g, Fat: 19 g, Protein: 5 g, Fiber: 2 g.

Ingredients:

- 1 large spaghetti squash
- 2 cups chopped mushrooms
- 1 ½ cups chopped spinach
- 1 tomato, chopped
- 1/2 cup white onion, peeled and diced
- 1 tablespoon chopped parsley
- 2 teaspoons minced garlic
- 1/2 teaspoons garlic powder
- 1 teaspoon salt
- ½ teaspoon ground black pepper
- 2 teaspoons Italian seasoning blend, organic
- 1 teaspoon crushed red pepper flakes
- 1/2 teaspoons dried basil
- 2 teaspoons olive oil
- 1 ½ cups ricotta cheese
- 2/3 cup grated parmesan cheese
- 2-ounce grated mozzarella cheese

- 1 egg white
- 1/2 cup spaghetti sauce

Method:
- Set oven to 400 degrees F and let preheat.

- In the meantime, cut the squash in half, then remove its seed and then brush oil on its flesh.

- Place squash halves on a baking sheet and place into the oven to bake for 40 minutes or until roasted and tender.

- Meanwhile, prepare your vegetables and set aside.

- Place a large skillet pan over medium-high heat, add oil and when heated, add onions.

- Let cook for 5 minutes or until nicely golden.

- Then stir in garlic and mushrooms and continue cooking for 3 to 5 minutes or until tender.

- When done, transfer onion mixture to a bowl and set aside.

- Place spinach in a bowl, add garlic powder, salt, black pepper, Italian seasoning, basil, ricotta and parmesan cheese and egg white.

- Add onion-mushroom mixture along with tomatoes and stir until well combined, set aside.

- When squash is done with cooking, let it cool slightly and then make spaghetti noodles from its flesh using a fork.

- Take a baking dish, grease with oil, add spaghetti squash and top with cheese and vegetable mixture.

- Mix until combined, then top with mozzarella cheese and sprinkle with red pepper flakes.

- Lower oven temperature to 350 degrees F, then place baking dish into the oven and let bake for 25 minutes.

- Then switch on the broiler and broil at high heat setting for 2 minutes or until top is nicely browned.

- When done, sprinkle with parsley and serve.

Day 12

Breakfast

Mexican Kale Frittata

| Servings: 4 |
| Preparation time: 15 minutes | Cooking time: 12 minutes | Total time: 27 minutes |

Nutrition Value:
Calories: 170 Cal, Carbs: 7 g, Net Carbs: 4 g, Fat: 8 g, Protein: 16 g, Fiber: 3 g.

Ingredients:

- 1 large kale bunch, stem removed, and leaves chopped

- ¼ cup baby spinach,

- 2 medium-sized tomatoes, quartered

- ½ a medium-sized red onion, peeled and chopped

- 1 teaspoon salt

- ¾ teaspoon ground black pepper

- 1 teaspoon paprika, organic

- 1-inch Feta cheese, sliced

- 4 eggs, slightly beaten

Method:
- Place a pan over high heat, add oil and when heated, add onions.

- Let cook for 1 minute or until softened, and then add kale and spinach.

- Stir and let cook for 2 minutes, and then season with salt, black pepper, and paprika.

- Crack eggs in a bowl, beat slightly and then spoon in cooked kale mixture along with tomatoes.

- Stir until well combined and let sit for 5 minutes.

- In the meantime, set the oven to 350 degrees F and let preheat.

- Grease pan with oil, add egg mixture, top with cheese and let cook for 1 minute at medium-low heat.

- Then transfer pan into the oven and let bake for 6 minutes or until cooked through.

- Switch on the broiler and broil for 2 minutes.

- Slice to serve.

Lunch

Three Cheese Quiche Stuffed Peppers

| Servings: 4 |
| Preparation time: 10 minutes | Cooking time: 50 minutes | Total time: 60 minutes |

Nutrition Value:
Calories: 245.5 Cal, Carbs: 7.1 g, Net Carbs: 5.97 g, Fat: 1 g, Protein: 17.84 g, Fiber: 1.13 g.

Ingredients:

- 2 medium-sized bell peppers, halved and cored
- ¼ teaspoon dried parsley
- ¼ cup baby spinach leaves
- 1 teaspoon garlic powder
- ½ cup ricotta cheese
- ½ cup and 2 tablespoons grated Parmesan cheese
- ½ cup grated mozzarella cheese
- 4 eggs

Method:
- Set oven to 375 degrees F and let preheat.
- In the meantime, prepared bell peppers.
- Place ricotta cheese, mozzarella cheese, and ½ cup parmesan cheese in a large bowl along with parsley, garlic powder and eggs and pulse using an electric immersion hand blender at high speed for 3 minutes or until well combined and smooth.
- Stuff this mixture into each bell pepper half, then top with spinach and stir slightly using a fork.
- Cover each stuffed pepper with aluminum foil, then place into a baking sheet and let bake for 35 to 45 minutes or until egg is set.

- Then carefully uncover peppers, sprinkle with remaining 2 tablespoons of parmesan cheese and return to oven.

- Switch on the broiler and let broil for 5 minutes or until top is nicely golden brown.

- Serve when ready.

Dinner

Zucchini Basil Soup

| Servings: 4 |
| Preparation time: 10 minutes | Cooking time: 30 minutes | Total time: 40 minutes |

Nutrition Value:

Calories: 164 Cal, Carbs: 5.83 g, Net Carbs: 4.54 g, Fat: 13.96 g, Protein: 3.86 g, Fiber: 1.29 g.

Ingredients:

- 1 tablespoon minced garlic
- 16-ounce zucchini, trimmed and diced
- 1/3 cup basil leaves
- 1/2 teaspoon salt
- 1/2 teaspoon ground black pepper
- 1 tablespoon olive oil
- 1/2 cup whipping cream
- 2 cups vegetable broth

Method:

- Place a large saucepan over medium heat, add oil and when heated, add garlic.
- Let cook for 1 minute or until fragrant and then add zucchini and season with salt and black pepper.
- Let cook for 5 minutes or until tender and then pour in vegetable stock.
- Simmer soup for 10 minutes.
- Then remove the pan from heat, add basil and let sit for 5 minutes or until basil leaves wilt completely.
- Blend soup using an electric hand immersion blender until smooth.
- Stir in cream, then season with salt and black pepper and serve.

Day 13

Breakfast

Tomato & Goat Cheese Quiche

| Servings: 1 omelet |
| Preparation time: 10 minutes | Cooking time: 25 minutes | Total time: 35 minutes |

Nutrition Value:
Calories: 311Cal, Carbs: 6 g, Net Carbs: 3.2 g, Fat: 21 g, Protein: 22.1 g, Fiber: 2.8 g.

Ingredients:

- 1 vegetarian low-carb pie crust

- 6 cherry tomatoes, cut into quarters

- 6 leaves of kale, stems removed, and leaves chopped

- 1 teaspoon salt

- ½ teaspoon ground black pepper

- 1/2 tablespoon arrowroot powder

- 1/4 cup basil leaves

- 2 tablespoons heavy whipping cream

- 3 eggs

- 7.1-ounce ricotta cheese

- 1/4 cup grated Parmesan cheese

- 3.5-ounce goat cheese, crumbled

Method:

- Set oven to 375 degrees F and let preheat.

- Place pie crust in one tart pan and set aside.

- Place ricotta and parmesan cheese in a bowl, add salt, black pepper, and eggs and let whisk until smooth.

- Place cream in another bowl and whisk in arrowroot powder or until blended.

- Then whisk this mixture into cheese mixture.

- Add kale and basil and stir until mixed.

- Spoon this mixture into the tart and then top with cheese and tomato pieces.

- Place tart into the oven and let bake for 30 minutes or until cooked through.

- Slice to serve.

Lunch

Zucchini & Mint Salad

| Servings: 1 omelet |
| Preparation time: 15 minutes | Cooking time: 0 minutes | Total time: 15 minutes |

Nutrition Value:
Calories: 88 Cal, Carbs: 5.3 g, Net Carbs: 3.5 g, Fat: 7.3 g, Protein: 1.9 g, Fiber: 1.7 g.

Ingredients:

- 2 large zucchinis

- ¾ teaspoon salt

- ½ teaspoon ground black pepper

- 1/4 teaspoon red Chile flakes

- 1 tablespoon chopped mint

- 2 tablespoons olive oil

- 1 teaspoon lemon zest

- 1 tablespoon lemon juice

Method:
- Cut ends of both sides of zucchini and then cut into thin ribbons using a vegetable peeler.

- Whisk together mint, oil and lemon juice until combined.

- Place zucchini ribbons in a bowl, season with salt and black pepper and add prepared dressing.

- Toss until coated and then sprinkle with chili flakes and lemon zest.

- Let salad chill in the refrigerator for 30 minutes before serving.

Dinner

Vegetable Soup

| Servings: 6 |
| Preparation time: 10 minutes | Cooking time: 25 minutes | Total time: 35 minutes |

Nutrition Value:
Calories: 258 Cal, Carbs: 8.3 g, Net Carbs: 5.6 g, Fat: 23.6 g, Protein: 4.4 g, Fiber: 2.7 g.

Ingredients:

- 1 ½ pounds cauliflower, cut into florets
- 1-pound zucchini
- 2 stalks of celery
- 1 teaspoon thyme leaves, and more for garnishing
- 1 small red onion, peeled and chopped
- 1/2 teaspoon onion powder
- 1 teaspoon minced garlic
- 1 teaspoon sea salt
- 1 teaspoon ground black pepper
- 2 tablespoons coconut oil
- 4 tablespoons olive oil
- 1 cup coconut cream, full-fat
- 2 cups vegetable stock
- 2 cups water

Method:
- Place a large saucepan over medium-high heat, add coconut oil and when melts, add onion and garlic.

- Add cauliflower florets, zucchini, celery, thyme, onion powder, garlic powder, salt and black pepper and stir until mixed.

- Pour in vegetable stock and water and bring the mixture to boil.

- Then simmer for 15 minutes or until vegetables are tender, covering the pan.

- Then remove the pan from heat and blend soup using an electric hand immersion blender until smooth.

- Stir in cream, then return pan to heat and let heat for 3 to 5 minutes or until heated through.

- Ladle soup into four serving bowls, drizzle with olive oil and serve.

Day 14

Breakfast

Cinnamon & Pecan Porridge

| Servings: 1 |

| Preparation time: 10 minutes | Cooking time: 10 minutes | Total time: 20 minutes |

Nutrition Value:

Calories: 580　Cal, Carbs: 15.7 g, Net Carbs: 5.2 g, Fat: 51.7 g, Protein: 13.8 g, Fiber: 10.5 g.

Ingredients:

- 2 tablespoons chia seeds

- 2 tablespoons hemp seeds

- 1/4 cup chopped pecans

- 1/4 cup toasted coconut, unsweetened

- 1/2 teaspoon ground cinnamon

- 1 tablespoon 1 teaspoon erythritol sweetener, granulated

- 1/4 cup almond butter

- 1 tablespoon coconut oil

- 1/4 cup coconut milk, full-fat and unsweetened

- 3/4 cup almond milk, full-fat and unsweetened

Method:

- Pour in coconut and almond milk in a saucepan and place over medium heat.

- Stir in butter and coconut oil and bring the mixture to simmer.

- Then remove the pan from heat and stir in seeds, pecans, coconut, cinnamon, and sweetener.

- Let sit for 10 minutes and then serve.

Lunch

Egg Stuffed Avocado

| Servings: 2 |
| Preparation time: 15 minutes | Cooking time: 0 minutes | Total time: 15 minutes |

Nutrition Value:
Calories: 616 Cal, Carbs: 15.3 g, Net Carbs: 4.8 g, Fat: 56.8 g, Protein: 16.5 g, Fiber: 10.6 g.

Ingredients:

- 2 medium-sized avocados, cored
- 2 medium spring onions, sliced and more for garnishing
- 1/4 teaspoon salt
- 1/4 teaspoon ground black pepper
- 1 teaspoon yellow mustard
- 4 eggs, boiled and peeled
- 1/4 cup mayonnaise, organic
- 2 tablespoons cream cheese, softened

Method:
- Dice boiled eggs and place in a bowl along with sliced onion, mustard, mayonnaise and cream cheese.
- Season with salt and black pepper.
- Using a spoon, scoop out flesh from avocado halve until 1-inch flesh is left.
- Then chop the scooped out avocado flesh, add to egg mixture and stir until well mixed.
- Stuff this mixture into avocado halves and top with green onions.
- Serve immediately.

Dinner

Vegetarian Burgers

| Servings: 2 burgers |
| Preparation time: 15 minutes | Cooking time: 20 minutes | Total time: 35 minutes |

Nutrition Value:
Calories: 637 Cal, Carbs: 18.8 g, Net Carbs: 8.7 g, Fat: 55.1 g, Protein: 23.7 g, Fiber: 10.1 g.

Ingredients:

- 2 medium Portobello mushrooms

- 2 slices of tomato

- 1 cup lettuce leaves

- 1 teaspoon minced garlic

- 1/4 teaspoon salt

- 1/4 teaspoon ground black pepper

- 2 tablespoons chopped basil

- 1 tablespoon chopped oregano

- 1 tablespoon coconut oil, melted

- 2 eggs

- 2 slices of cheddar cheese

- 2 low carb buns

- 2 tablespoons mayonnaise, organic

Method:
- Season mushrooms with garlic, salt, and black pepper, then sprinkle with basil and oregano and drizzle with coconut oil.

- Let mushrooms marinate for 30 minutes at room temperature.

- Place a griddle pan over medium-high heat, grease with oil and when heated, add marinated mushrooms, top side up.

- Let cook for 5 minutes per side and then place a cheese slice over cut side of the mushroom.

- Place mushrooms in a broiler and let broil for 3 to 5 minutes at high heat setting or until cheese melts.

- In the meantime, fry eggs, one at a time, or until cooked to desired liking.

- Cut buns in half and let heat on a griddle pan until crispy on both sides.

- Working on one burger at a time, first spread mayonnaise on bottom half of bun, top with a mushroom, then fried egg, a tomato slices, and lettuce leaves.

- Cover with top half of bun and serve.

Day 15

Breakfast

McMuffins

| Servings: 1 |
| Preparation time: 10 minutes | Cooking time: 2 minutes | Total time: 12 minutes |

Nutrition Value:
Calories: 626 Cal, Carbs: 9.4 g, Net Carbs: 2.9 g, Fat: 54.6 g, Protein: 26.5 g, Fiber: 6.5 g.

Ingredients:

For Muffin

- 1/4 cup almond flour

- 1/4 cup flax meal

- ¼ teaspoon salt

- 1/4 teaspoon baking soda

- 1 egg

- 1/4 cup grated cheddar cheese

- 2 tablespoons coconut milk, full-fat and unsweetened

- 2 tablespoons water

For Filling

- 1 slice of tomato

- 4 leaves of basil

- 1 teaspoon yellow mustard

- ½ teaspoon salt

- ½ teaspoon ground black pepper

- 1 tablespoon olive oil

- 2 tablespoons cream cheese, softened

- 2 slices of cheddar cheese

- 1 egg

Method:
- Place flour, flax meal, salt and baking powder in a bowl and stir until mixed.

- Add egg, water, and cream and stir until combined.

- Stir in cheese and then spoon this mixture into a ramekin.

- Place ramekin into the oven and let microwave for 60 to 90 seconds at high heat setting or until done.

- In the meantime, fry eggs until cooked to desired liking.

- Then season eggs with salt and black pepper and transfer eggs to a plate.

- When muffin is cooked through, take it out from ramekin, let cool it slightly and then cut in half.

- Spread cream cheese on one side of each half, then layer with cheese slices.

- Top with fried egg, tomato slice, basil and drizzle with mustard.

- Top with over half of muffin and serve.

Lunch

Cottage Cheese Roast

| Servings: 2 |
| Preparation time10 10 minutes | Cooking time: 40 minutes | Total time: 50 minutes |

Nutrition Value:
Calories: 278 Cal, Carbs: 6 g, Net Carbs: 4.7 g, Fat: 21.5 g, Protein: 12.9 g, Fiber: 1.3 g.

Ingredients:

- 1 1/2 cups cornflakes cereal
- 2 tablespoons dry onion soup mix
- 1 cup chopped walnuts
- 1/4 cup olive oil
- 16-ounce creamed cottage cheese
- 4 eggs, slightly beaten

Method:
- Set oven to 350 degrees F and let preheat.
- Place all the ingredients in a bowl and stir until well combined.
- Take a loaf pan, grease with non-stick cooking spray and spoon in prepared cheese mixture.
- Place loaf pan into the oven and let bake for 40 minutes or until done and the top is nicely browned.
- Take out cheese from loaf pan, cut into bite size pieces and serve.

Dinner

Spinach Pie

| Servings: 1 pie |
| Preparation time: 10 minutes | Cooking time: 25 minutes | Total time: 35 minutes |

Nutrition Value:
Calories: 501 Cal, Carbs: 9.1 g, Net Carbs: 5.6 g, Fat: 47.1 g, Protein: 14.4 g, Fiber: 3.5 g.

Ingredients:

- 16-ounce frozen chopped spinach, thawed and moisture squeezed out

- 2 tablespoons chopped onion

- 2 tablespoons vegetarian butter

- ½ teaspoon salt

- ½ teaspoon ground black pepper

- ½ teaspoon ground nutmeg

- 1 1/2 cups coconut cream

- 3 eggs

- ½ cup shredded Swiss cheese

Method:
- Set oven to 375 degrees and let preheat.

- Place a large saucepan over medium-high heat, add butter and when melts, add onion.

- Let cook for 3 minutes or until softened and then add spinach.

- Let cook for 3 to 5 minutes or until moisture evaporate and spinach is heated through.

- In the meantime, crack eggs in a bowl and whisk in salt, black pepper, nutmeg, and cream.

- Grease a 99-inch pie pan with oil, then spoon in cooked spinach and spread cream mixture evenly on top.

- Sprinkle with cheese and let bake for 30 minutes or until top is nicely golden brown.

- When done, let the pie cool for 5 minutes and then slice to serve.

Day 16

Breakfast

Carrot & Thyme Loaf

| Servings: 1 loaf |
| Preparation time: 10 minutes | Cooking time: 45 minutes | Total time: 55 minutes |

Nutrition Value:
Calories: 405 Cal, Carbs: 17.3 g, Net Carbs: 8.8 g, Fat: 33.7 g, Protein: 12.7 g, Fiber: 8.5 g.

Ingredients:

- 4 tablespoons flaxseeds, grounded

- 3 tablespoons sunflower seeds

- 4 tablespoons pumpkin seeds

- 4 carrots

- 1 teaspoon sea salt

- 2 tablespoons chopped thyme, fresh

- 1 tablespoon sesame oil

- 3 tablespoons olive oil

- 2 eggs

Method:

- Set oven to 375 degrees F and let preheat.

- Grate carrot and place in a bowl along with remaining ingredients except for sesame oil.

- Stir until well incorporated and spoon this mixture into a greased loaf pan.

- Place loaf pan into the oven and let make for 40 to 45 minutes or until top is nicl4ey golden brown and inserted toothpick into the center of the loaf comes out clean.

- When done, take out loaf, then drizzle with sesame oil and slice to serve.

Lunch

Italian Cheese Stuffed Mushrooms

| Servings: 4 |
| Preparation time: 15 minutes | Cooking time: 20 minutes | Total time: 35 minutes |

Nutrition Value:
Calories: 432 Cal, Carbs: 13.5 g, Net Carbs: 8.9 g, Fat: 36.8 g, Protein: 22.8 g, Fiber: 4.6 g.

Ingredients:

- 8 Portobello mushrooms, cored
- 10-ounce frozen kale, drained and moisture squeezed
- 2 tablespoons red bell pepper, diced
- 1/2 small red onion, peeled and chopped
- 1/8 teaspoons dried Italian herbs
- 1/2 teaspoon minced garlic
- 2 tablespoons vegetarian butter, unsalted
- 1/2 cup grated Parmesan
- 1/4 cup grated cheddar cheese and more for garnishing
- 1 cup cream cheese
- 1/4 cup ricotta cheese
- 3.5-ounces goat's cheese

Method:

- Set oven to 355 degrees F and let preheat.
- Remove stems and gills in mushrooms, rinse and pat dry completely and then brush with butter.
- Place these mushroom caps on a baking tray and set aside.

- Chop spinach and add to a bowl along with onion, garlic, and all cheeses.

- Mix until well combined and then stuff this mixture into mushroom caps.

- Garnish with red pepper and cheddar cheese and let bake for 20 minutes or until top is browned.

- When done, sprinkle with Italian herbs and serve.

Dinner

Cheese Curry

| Servings: 2 |
| Preparation time: 10 minutes | Cooking time: 25 minutes | Total time: 35 minutes |

Nutrition Value:
Calories: 458 Cal, Carbs: 10.2 g, Net Carbs: 7.8 g, Fat: 40.4 g, Protein: 15.6 g, Fiber: 2.4 g.

Ingredients:

- 7-ounces cottage cheese, fresh and cubed

- 1/2 of a large white onion, peeled and chopped

- 2 medium tomatoes, chopped

- 2 tablespoons coriander

- 1 teaspoon minced garlic

- ½ teaspoon grated ginger

- 1 teaspoon salt

- ½ teaspoon turmeric powder

- ¼ teaspoon garam masala

- 1/2 teaspoon cumin seeds

- ½ tablespoon tomato paste 3 tablespoons olive oil

- 1 bay leaf

- 1/3 cup coconut cream, full-fat

- 1/3 cup water

Method:
- Place a large pan over medium-high heat, add oil and when heated, add cumin and bay leaf.

- Let cook for 1 minute or until fragrant and then add onion, garlic, and ginger.

- Switch heat to medium-low and let cook for 10 minutes or until onion is tender.

- Add tomatoes and tomato paste, and stir in salt, turmeric, coriander powder, and water.

- Let cook for 5 minutes and remove bay leaf.

- Transfer mixture into a blender and pulse until smooth.

- Return this sauce to the pan at medium-high heat, add cheese and let simmer for 5 minutes.

- Then remove the pan from heat, stir in garam masala and cream.

- Garnish with coriander and serve.

Day 17

Breakfast

Quesadilla

| Servings: 3 Quesadilla |
| Preparation time: 10 minutes | Cooking time: 25 minutes | Total time: 35 minutes |

Nutrition Value:
Calories: 473 Cal, Carbs: 8 g, Net Carbs: 5 g, Fat: 41 g, Protein: 21 g, Fiber: 3 g.

Ingredients:

- 1-ounce leafy greens
- 1 tablespoon coconut flour
- 1 ½ teaspoon ground husk powder
- ½ teaspoon salt
- 6-ounce cream cheese
- 5-ounce grated Mexican cheese
- 1 tablespoon olive oil
- 2 eggs
- 2 egg whites

Method:

- Set oven to 400 degrees F and let preheat.
- In the meantime, place egg and egg white in a bowl and blend using an electric hand immersion blender until fluffy.
- Then beat in cream cheese until smooth.
- Place flour in another bowl, add husk powder along with salt and mix well.
- Stir this flour mixture gradually into egg mixture until incorporated and then let the batter rest for 10 minutes.

- Take a baking sheet, line with parchment paper and then spread prepared quesadilla batter in the square on it.

- Place the baking sheet into the oven and let bake for 5 to 7 minutes or until edges start to brown.

- When done, cut quesadilla into 6 pieces.

- Place a skillet pan over medium heat, add oil and when heated, add one quesadilla slice.

- Sprinkle cheese on top, scatter with greens and over with another quesadilla.

- Let cook for 1 to 2 minutes per side or until cheese melt completely.

- Cook remaining quesadilla in the same manner and serve.

Lunch

Chile-Lime Spiced Almonds

| Servings: 4 |
| Preparation time: 10 minutes | Cooking time: 25 minutes | Total time: 35 minutes |

Nutrition Value:
Calories: 241 Cal, Carbs: 8.5 g, Net Carbs: 3.7 g, Fat: 21.3 g, Protein: 7.7 g, Fiber: 4.7 g.

Ingredients:

- 2 cups almonds

- 1/4 teaspoon garlic powder

- 1/2 teaspoon onion powder

- 1 teaspoon sea salt

- 1 teaspoon red chili powder

- 1/2 teaspoon smoked paprika, organic

- 2 teaspoons fresh lime zest

- 2 tablespoons olive oil

- 2 tablespoons lime juice

Method:
- Set oven to 340 degrees F and let preheat.

- Place all the ingredients in a bowl and stir until mixed.

- Let almonds marinate for 10 minutes and then spread in a single layer on a baking tray, lined with parchment paper.

- Place the baking tray into the oven and let bake for 20 to 25 minutes.

- When done, let almonds cool and then serve.

Dinner

Pumpkin Soup

| Servings: 4 |
| Preparation time: 10 minutes | Cooking time: 35 minutes | Total time: 45 minutes |

Nutrition Value:
Calories: 865 Cal, Carbs: 17 g, Net Carbs: 14 g, Fat: 88 g, Protein: 6 g, Fiber: 3 g.

Ingredients:

- 10-ounce pumpkins, peeled and cubed
- 10-ounces rutabaga, peeled and cubed
- 4 tablespoons pumpkin seeds, roasted
- 2 shallots, peeled and diced
- 2 cloves of garlic, peeled
- 1 teaspoon salt
- ½ teaspoon ground black pepper
- 1 tablespoon lime juice
- 2 tablespoons olive oil
- 1 cup vegetarian butter, cubed
- ¾ cup mayonnaise, organic
- 2 cups vegetable stock

Method:

- Set oven to 400 degrees F and let preheat.
- Place pumpkin, rutabaga, shallots, and garlic in a baking dish, drizzle with oil and season with salt and black pepper.
- Toss to coat and let roast for 25 to 30 minutes or until tender.

- Then transfer these vegetables into the pot, then pour in vegetable stock and place pot over medium heat.

- Bring the mixture to boil and then simmer for 5 minutes.

- Remove pot from heat and stir in butter cubes.

- Puree soup using an electric immersion hand blender.

- Stir in salt, black pepper, and lemon juice and ladle soup into bowls.

- Top with mayonnaise and pumpkin seeds and serve.

Day 18

Breakfast

Pesto Egg Muffins

| Servings: 10 Muffins |
| Preparation time: 5 minutes | Cooking time: 25 minutes | Total time: 30 minutes |

Nutrition Value:
Calories: 125 Cal, Carbs: 1.9 g, Net Carbs: 1.2 g, Fat: 10.2 g, Protein: 6.9 g, Fiber: 0.7 g.

Ingredients:

- 1/2 cup kalamata olives, pitted and sliced

- 1/4 cup sun-dried tomatoes, chopped

- 2/3 cup frozen spinach, thawed moisture squeezed

- 1 ½ teaspoon salt

- 1 teaspoon ground black pepper

- 3 tablespoons basil pesto, fresh

- 6 eggs

- 4.4-ounces feta cheese

Method:

- Set oven to 350 degrees F and let preheat.

- Place olives, tomatoes, and spinach in a bowl and stir until combined.

- Crack eggs in another bowl and whisk in pesto, salt, and black pepper.

- Grease a six cups muffin tray with non-stick cooking spray, evenly fill with vegetable mixture and then pour in egg mixture until filled.

- Place muffin tray into the oven and let bake for 20 to 25 minutes or until top is nicely brown and muffins are cooked through.

- When done, take out the muffin, let cool slightly and then serve.

Lunch

Zucchini Fritters

| Servings: 4 |
| Preparation time: 10 minutes | Cooking time: 15 minutes | Total time: 25 minutes |

Nutrition Value:
Calories: 216 Cal, Carbs: 5 g, Net Carbs: 3.2 g, Fat: 19.8 g, Protein: 6.3 g, Fiber: 1.8 g.

Ingredients:

- 1/4 cup almond flour

- 3 medium zucchinis, grated

- 1 teaspoon sea salt

- 1/4 teaspoon ground black pepper

- 1/4 cup olive oil

- 1 egg

- 1/4 cup grated Parmesan cheese

Method:
- Place grated zucchini in a cheesecloth, wrap it and squeeze tightly to drain moisture completely.

- Then place zucchini in a bowl, add remaining ingredients except for oil and stir until well mixed.

- Shape mixture into 8 patties and set aside.

- Place a skillet pan over medium-high heat, add oil and when heated, add patties in a single layer.

- Let cook for 3 to 4 minutes per side or until nicely golden browned and crispy on all sides.

- Serve when ready.

Dinner

Cabbage Casserole

| Servings: 6 |
| Preparation time: 10 minutes | Cooking time: 40 minutes | Total time: 50 minutes |

Nutrition Value:

Calories: 527 Cal, Carbs: 13 g, Net Carbs: 11 g, Fat: 49 g, Protein: 11 g, Fiber: 4 g.

Ingredients:

- 30-ounce green cabbage

- 1 medium-sized white onion

- 2 cloves of garlic, peeled

- 1 teaspoon salt

- ½ teaspoon ground black pepper

- 1 tablespoon ranch seasoning

- 15 teaspoons sour cream, organic and full-fat

- 5 1/3-ounce cream cheese

- 3-ounce vegetarian butter

- 1¼ cups coconut cream, full-fat

- 5 1/3-ounce grated parmesan cheese

Method:

- Set oven to 400 degrees F and let preheat.

- In the meantime, cut the cabbage into wedges and add to a food processor along with onion and garlic and process until finely chopped.

- Place a large frying pan over medium heat, add butter and when melts, add vegetables.

- Let cook for 8 to 10 minutes or until softened.

- Then stir in salt, black pepper, ranch seasoning, sour cream, cream cheese and coconut cream.

- Let mixture simmer for 7 to 10 minutes and then add to a baking dish, greased with non-stick cooking spray.

- Sprinkle cheese on top, the place baking dish into the oven and let bake for 20 minutes or until cheese melts and the top is nicely golden brown.

- Serve when ready.

Day 19

Breakfast

Mushroom Omelet

| Servings: 1 omelet |
| Preparation time: 4 minutes | Cooking time: 6 minutes | Total time: 10 minutes |

Nutrition Value:
Calories: 510Cal, Carbs: 5 g, Net Carbs: 4 g, Fat: 43 g, Protein: 25 g, Fiber: 1 g.

Ingredients:

- 3 mushrooms

- 2 tablespoons chopped white onion

- ½ teaspoon salt

- ½ teaspoon ground black pepper

- 2 tablespoons vegetarian butter

- 2 tablespoons grated parmesan cheese

- 3 eggs

Method:

- Crack eggs in a bowl, add salt and black pepper and whisk until smooth.

- Place a frying pan over medium heat, add butter and when melts, pour in egg batter.

- Let cook for 2 to 3 minutes or until edges start to firm.

- Then scatter onion, mushroom, and cheese on top and then fold it over in half.

- Let cook for 2 to 3 minutes or until the bottom is nicely golden brown.

- Then slide omelet to a serving plate and serve.

Lunch

Tofu Salad

| Servings: 2 |
| Preparation time: 10 minutes | Cooking time: 15 minutes | Total time: 25 minutes |

Nutrition Value:
Calories: 486 Cal, Carbs: 34 g, Net Carbs: 27.3 g, Fat: 32 g, Protein: 29 g, Fiber: 6.7 g.

Ingredients:

- 14-ounces firm tofu, pressed and drained

- 2 tablespoons peanuts

- 8-ounce diced pineapple, cubed

- ½ of a medium cucumber, de-seeded and cubed

- ¼ cup spinach

- ½ of a jalapeño pepper, finely chopped

- 1 cup bean sprouts

- ½ of a bunch of radishes, peeled and sliced

- 1 teaspoon salt

- ¾ teaspoon ground black pepper

- 1 tablespoon erythritol, powdered

- 1 teaspoon Sriracha sauce, organic

- 1 tablespoon lemon juice

- 3 tablespoons olive oil

Method:
- Cut pressed tofu into small pieces.

- Place a pan over medium heat, add 1 tablespoon oil and when heat, add tofu.

- Let cook for 15 minutes or until nicely golden brown on all sides.

- In the meantime, prepare vegetables and place them in a bowl.

- In another bowl whisk together salt, black pepper, erythritol, Sriracha, lemon juice and remaining oil until combined.

- Add to vegetables and toss to coat.

- When tofu is done, divide evenly among serving plates, top with vegetables and garnish with pepper and peanuts.

- Serve immediately.

Dinner

Grilled Halloumi Salad

| Servings: 1 |
| Preparation time: 10 minutes | Cooking time: 25 minutes | Total time: 35 minutes |

Nutrition Value:
Calories: 560 Cal, Carbs: 7 g, Net Carbs: 5.7 g, Fat: 47 g, Protein: 21 g, Fiber: 2.3 g.

Ingredients:

- 1 medium-sized cucumber, sliced

- 5 cherry tomatoes, halved

- ¼ cup baby arugula

- 1/3 teaspoon salt

- 1 tablespoon chopped walnuts

- 1 tablespoon olive oil

- 1 tablespoon apple cider vinegar, organic

- 3-ounces halloumi cheese

Method:

- Place a griddle pan over medium heat, grease with oil and let preheat.

- In the meantime, slice cheese into 1/3-inch-thick pieces and add to griddle pan.

- Let cook for 3 to 5 minutes per side.

- In the meantime, prepared vegetables and place in a large bowl.

- When cheese is done, top it on salad and sprinkle with salt.

- Drizzle with oil and vinegar, toss to coat and serve.

Day 20

Breakfast

Spinach Artichoke Breakfast Casserole

| Servings: 10 |
| Preparation time: 10 minutes | Cooking time: 6 hours | Total time: 6 hours and 10 minutes |

Nutrition Value:
Calories: 141 Cal, Carbs: 7.76 g, Net Carbs: 3.79 g, Fat: 7.1 g, Protein: 9.98 g, Fiber: 3.97 g.

Ingredients:

- ¾ cup coconut flour
- 5 ounces fresh spinach, chopped
- 6 ounces artichoke hearts, chopped
- 2 tablespoons chopped basil
- 1 ½ teaspoon minced garlic
- 1 teaspoon salt
- 1/2 teaspoon ground black pepper
- 1 tablespoon baking powder
- 8 eggs
- 3/4 cup almond milk, full-fat and unsweetened
- 1 cup grated parmesan cheese

Method:
- Place spinach and artichoke hearts in a large bowl, add salt, black pepper, eggs, milk and ½ cup cheese/
- Whisk until well combined and stir in flour and baking powder until incorporated.

- Grease a 6-quarts slow cooker with non-stick cooking spray, spoon in prepared batter and then sprinkle remaining cheese on top.

- Plug in the slow cooker, cover with its lid and let cook for 2 to 3 hours at high heat setting or until cooked through.

- When done, sprinkle with basil and serve.

Lunch

Kale Slaw

| Servings: 6 |
| Preparation time: 10 minutes | Cooking time: 0 minutes | Total time: 10 minutes |

Nutrition Value:
Calories: 147 Cal, Carbs: 6 g, Net Carbs: 3.5 g, Fat: 13.3 g, Protein: 3.4 g, Fiber: 2.5 g.

Ingredients:

- 2 1/2 cups grated red cabbage
- 6-ounces kale, stem removed, and leaves sliced
- 1 1/4 cups grated green cabbage
- 1/2 cup grated carrot
- ¾ teaspoon salt
- ½ teaspoon ground black pepper
- 1/4 cup pumpkin seeds
- 1 tablespoon apple cider vinegar, organic
- 1/3 cup mayonnaise, organic

Method:
- Place kale, carrot, and cabbages in a bowl and toss until mixed.
- Whisk together remaining ingredients except for pumpkin seeds in another bowl and then drizzle this dressing over salad.
- Toss to coat, top with pumpkin seeds and serve.

Dinner

Broccoli & Leek Soup

| Servings: 4 |
| Preparation time: 15 minutes | Cooking time: 10 minutes | Total time: 25 minutes |

Nutrition Value:
Calories: 504 Cal, Carbs: 11 g, Net Carbs: 8 g, Fat: 47 g, Protein: 13 g, Fiber: 8 g.

Ingredients:

- 10-ounces broccoli

- 1 leek, chopped

- 1 teaspoon minced garlic

- ¾ teaspoon salt

- ½ teaspoon ground black pepper

- 25 teaspoon fresh basil leaves

- ½ cup olive oil

- 3 cups water

- 8-ounce cream cheese

Method:

- Cut off core from broccoli, slice it thinly and cut remaining broccoli into florets.

- Place sliced broccoli core in a pot along with leek and pour in water.

- Stir in salt and bring to boil over high heat or until broccoli core is tender.

- Lower heat to low heat, add garlic and broccoli florets and let simmer for 5 minutes or until florets are tender.

- Remove pot from heat, then add remaining ingredients and puree the soup using an electric hand immersion blender until smooth.

- Ladle soup into bowls and serve with egg muffins.

Day 21

Breakfast

Hemp Heart Porridge

| Servings: 1 |
| Preparation time: 2 minutes | Cooking time: 3 minutes | Total time: 5 minutes |

Nutrition Value:
Calories: 867 Cal, Carbs: 26.8 g, Net Carbs: 2.3 g, Fat: 72.8 g, Protein: 43.8 g, Fiber: 24.5 g.

Ingredients:

- ½ cup and 1 tablespoon Hemp Hearts
- ¼ cup almond flour
- 1 tablespoon chia seeds
- 2 tablespoons ground flax seed
- 3 Brazil nuts
- 1 tablespoon erythritol, granulated
- ½ teaspoon ground cinnamon
- ¾ teaspoon vanilla extract, unsweetened
- 1 cup almond milk, full-fat and unsweetened

Method:
- Place a saucepan over medium heat and add ½ cup Hemp hearts along with all the ingredients except for almond flour and Brazil nuts.
- Let cook until begin to boil and continue cooking for another 2 minutes.
- Then remove the pan from heat, stir in almond flour and transfer to a serving bowl.
- Top with Brazil nuts and hemp seeds and serve with fruits.

Lunch

Cream of Broccoli & Coconut Soup

| Servings: 4 |
| Preparation time: 10 minutes | Cooking time: 30 minutes | Total time: 40 minutes |

Nutrition Value:
Calories: 311 Cal, Carbs: 11.1 g, Net Carbs: 8 g, Fat: 29.5 g, Protein: 4.8 g, Fiber: 3 g.

Ingredients:

- 2 shallots, peeled and diced
- 10.6-ounce broccoli, cut in florets
- ¼ cup watercress
- 1 tablespoon pumpkin seeds
- 1 tablespoon sunflower seeds
- 1/3 cup grated coconut
- 2 teaspoons minced garlic
- 1/3 teaspoon salt
- 1/4 teaspoon ground black pepper
- 2 tablespoons coconut oil
- 1 tablespoon olive oil
- 2 tablespoons coconut cream
- 4 cups vegetable stock
- 3/4 cup coconut milk, full-fat and unsweetened

Method:
- Pour stock in a saucepan, place it over medium heat and let simmer for 20 minutes or until reduced by half.

- In the meantime, place another saucepan over medium heat, add 1 tablespoon coconut oil and when heated, add onion.

- Let cook for 2 minutes or until tender, then add garlic and cook for another minute or until fragrant.

- When done, remove the pan from heat.

- Add broccoli florets into reduced stock, then remove the pan from heat and let stand for 10 minutes.

- Then return pan over medium heat, add shallots, stir in garlic, salt, and black pepper, pour in coconut milk and let cook for 2 to 3 minutes or until heated through.

- Remove pan from heat and puree soup using an electric immersion hand blender until smooth.

- Add remaining coconut oil, coconut cream, and watercress and puree again until blended.

- Return pan to heat and let cook until heated through.

- Then ladle soup into bowls, drizzle with olive oil, and sprinkle with grated coconut, hemp, and sunflower seeds and serve.

Dinner

Mediterranean Salad

| Servings: 6 |
| Preparation time: 10 minutes | Cooking time: 0 minutes | Total time: 10 minutes |

Nutrition Value:
Calories: 155 Cal, Carbs: 9 g, Net Carbs: 7 g, Fat: 12 g, Protein: 4 g, Fiber: 2 g.

Ingredients:

- 2 cup cherry tomatoes, halved
- 2 cup cucumbers, de-seeded and chopped
- 1 cup artichoke hearts, chopped
- 1/3 cup red onion, peeled and sliced
- 1/2 cup feta cheese, crumbled
- 1 cup leafy greens

For Dressing

- 2 tablespoons sun-dried tomatoes
- 1/4 teaspoon sea salt
- 1/8 teaspoon ground black pepper
- 1 clove garlic
- 4 teaspoons apple cider vinegar, organic
- 6 tablespoons olive oil

Method:
- Place all the ingredients for dressing in a food processor and pulse until smooth.
- Place salad ingredients in a bowl, add dressing and toss to coat.
- Taste to adjust seasoning and serve.

Day 22

Breakfast

Avocado Toast

| Servings: 2 toasts |
| Preparation time: 15 minutes | Cooking time: 45 minutes | Total time: 60 minutes |

Nutrition Value:
Calories: 350 Cal, Carbs: 5.5 g, Net Carbs: 3.5 g, Fat: 32 g, Protein: 10 g, Fiber: 2 g.

Ingredients:

For Bread

- 2 cups almond flour
- 1/2 teaspoon xanthan gum
- 1/2 teaspoon sea salt
- 1 teaspoon baking powder
- 1/2 cup vegetarian butter, melted
- 7 eggs
- 2 tablespoons coconut oil, melted

For Avocado Topping

- 1 medium avocado, peeled and cored
- 2 tablespoons sunflower seeds
- ½ teaspoon sea salt

Method:
- First, prepare bread by setting the oven to 350 degrees F and let preheat.
- Crack eggs in a bowl and whisk using an electric immersion hand blender for 2 minutes at high speed or until frothy.

- Beat in melted butter and oil along with remaining ingredients for bread, one at a time.

- Spoon batter into a loaf pan, lined with parchment paper and place pan into the oven.

- Let bake for 45 minutes or until top is nicely browned and inserted a skewer into the bread comes out clean.

- When the bread is baked, take it out from loaf pan, then let cool slightly and then cut out two bread slices.

- Peel avocado, remove its pit and slice thinly.

- Place slices of one half of avocado on one slice of bread and spread other slices of avocado on another slice of bread.

- Sprinkle salt over avocado slices and sunflower seeds and serve.

Lunch

Garlic & Parmesan Fried Zucchini

| Servings: 6 |
| Preparation time: 15 minutes | Cooking time: 20 minutes | Total time: 35 minutes |

Nutrition Value:
Calories: 233 Cal, Carbs: 6.5 g, Net Carbs: 4.3 g, Fat: 16.7 g, Protein: 14.3 g, Fiber: 2.2 g.

Ingredients:

- 4 tablespoon coconut flour

- 2 medium zucchinis, sliced

- 1/2 teaspoon garlic powder

- 1/2 teaspoon sea salt

- 1/2 teaspoon paprika, organic

- 1/2 teaspoon Italian seasoning, organic

- 6 tablespoons coconut oil

- 2 eggs

- 1 1/2 cups grated Parmesan cheese

Method:
- Crack eggs in one bowl and whisk until frothy.

- Place cheese in another bowl.

- Place coconut flour in another bowl, add garlic powder, salt, paprika and Italian seasoning and stir until mixed.

- Place a skillet pan over medium-high heat, add oil and let heat.

- Working on one zucchini slice at a time, first coat with flour with coconut flour mixture, then dip into egg and coat with cheese and add to skillet pan.

- Fill pan with more zucchini slices, coated in the same manner and let cook for 1 to 2 minutes per side or until nicely golden brown.

- When cooked, transfer zucchini chips to plate towels and then serve with favorite dip.

Dinner

Ratatouille

| Servings: 3 |
| Preparation time: 30 minutes | Cooking time: 45 minutes | Total time: 1 hour and 15 minutes |

Nutrition Value:
Calories: 150.8 Cal, Carbs: 10.5 g, Net Carbs: 5.9 g, Fat: 12.3 g, Protein2.2 1 g, Fiber: 4.6 g.

Ingredients:

- 1 eggplant, unpeeled

- 1 medium zucchini

- 1 medium summer squash, cored and chopped

- 1 small sweet red peppers, diced

- 1 small tomatoes, diced

- 1 small white onions, peeled and sliced

- 2 teaspoons minced garlic

- 1 teaspoon salt

- 1/4 teaspoon black pepper

- 1/2 teaspoon dried rosemary

- 1/2 tablespoon dried thyme

- 1/3 olive oil

Method:
- Cut eggplant into thin slices, lengthwise, then sprinkle with salt and let rest for 20 minutes into a colander or until all its moisture is a drain.

- Then rinse eggplant slices and pat dry.

- Set oven to 425 degrees F and let preheat.

- Place all the ingredients in a baking dish, toss until well mixed and then cover with aluminum foil.

- Place baking dish into the oven and let bake for 15 minutes.

- Then carefully uncover baking dish and continue baking for another 30 minutes or until vegetables are nicely browned and cooked through, stirring occasionally.

- Serve when ready.

Day 23

Breakfast

Garlic Bread

| Servings: 16 |
| Preparation time: 15 minutes | Cooking time: 5 minutes | Total time: 20 minutes |

Nutrition Value:
Calories: 194 Cal, Carbs: 7.3 g, Net Carbs: 2.6 g, Fat: 16.4 g, Protein: 7.2 g, Fiber: 4.7 g.

Ingredients:

- 16 small low-carb baguettes or buns

For Garlic & Herb Butter:

- 2 tablespoons chopped parsley
- 3 teaspoons minced garlic
- 1/2 teaspoon salt
- 1/4 teaspoon ground black pepper
- 2 tablespoon olive oil
- 1/2 cup vegetarian butter, softened

For Topping:

- ½ cup grated Parmesan cheese
- 2 tablespoons parsley
- Olive oil as needed for drizzling

Method:
- Set oven to 400 degrees F and let preheat.
- Cut each baguette or bun in half and set aside.
- Place all the ingredients for herb butter in a bowl and stir until well mixed.

- Spread this mixture over each half of baguette or bun and then sprinkle evenly with parmesan cheese.

- Arrange baguettes or buns in a large baking sheet and let bake for 5 minutes or until cheese melts and baguettes or buns are crispy.

- Sprinkle with parsley, then drizzle with oil and serve.

Lunch

Chili-Lime Roasted Butternut Salad

| Servings: 1 |
| Preparation time: 15 minutes | Cooking time: 25 minutes | Total time: 40 minutes |

Nutrition Value:
Calories: 239 Cal, Carbs: 21 g, Net Carbs: 16 g, Fat: 16 g, Protein: 8 g, Fiber: 5 g.

Ingredients:

- 1/4 cup toasted pumpkin seeds

- 2 pounds butternut squash, peeled and cored

- 2 romaine lettuce, leaves torn

- 1/3 cup chopped cilantro

- 2 teaspoons salt, divided

- 1 1/2 teaspoon ground black pepper, divided

- 1 teaspoon red chili powder

- 3/4 teaspoon erythritol, powdered

- 1/4 cup olive oil, divided

- 3 tablespoons lime juice

- 3/4 cup crumbled feta cheese

Method:
- Set oven to 400 degrees F and let preheat.

- Cut squash into 1-inch pieces and place in a single layer on a rimmed baking sheet.

- Drizzle with 1 tablespoon oil and sprinkle with 1 ½ salt, 1 teaspoon black pepper and chili powder.

- Place the baking sheet into the oven and let bake for 20 to 25 minutes or until squash is tender and nicely golden brown.

- In the meantime, whisk together cilantro, remaining oil, lime juice, erythritol, salt and black pepper.

- To assemble the salad, place lettuce leaves onto serving platter, top with roasted squash, scatter pumpkin seeds and cheese on top and drizzle with prepared cilantro dressing.

- Serve immediately.

Dinner

Cream of Mushroom Soup

| Servings: 5 |
| Preparation time: 10 minutes | Cooking time: 15 minutes | Total time: 25 minutes |

Nutrition Value:
Calories: 118 Cal, Carbs: 1.9 g, Net Carbs: 1.3 g, Fat: 12.5 g, Protein: 0.8 g, Fiber: 0.6 g.

Ingredients:

- 1 1/2 cups mushrooms, cooked and chopped
- 1 teaspoon dry minced onion
- 1/8 teaspoon dried thyme
- 1/4 teaspoon salt
- 1/4 teaspoon ground black pepper
- 1/2 teaspoon guar gum
- 1 tablespoon white cooking wine
- 1 tablespoon vegetarian butter
- 14 ounces vegetable broth
- 1/2 cup coconut cream
- 1/2 cup almond milk, full-fat and unsweetened

Method:
- Place mushrooms in a saucepan, add onion and thyme and then pour in broth.
- Place pan over medium heat and let cook for 10 to 15 minutes or until cooked through.
- Then stir in butter and guar gum and remove the pan from heat.
- Puree soup using an electric immersion hand blender.

- Stir in salt, black pepper, wine, milk, and cream until well combined.
- Taste to adjust seasoning and serve.

Day 24

Breakfast

Scrambled Tofu

| Servings: 1 omelet |
| Preparation time: 10 minutes | Cooking time: 6 minutes | Total time: 16 minutes |

Nutrition Value:
Calories: 190 Cal, Carbs: 9.7 g, Net Carbs: 7.3 g, Fat: 11.5 g, Protein: 12 g, Fiber: 2.4 g.

Ingredients:

- 12-ounces firm tofu, pressed and drained
- 1 bunch green onions, chopped
- 14.5-ounces tomatoes, peeled and juiced
- ½ teaspoon salt
- ½ teaspoon ground black pepper
- ¼ teaspoon ground turmeric to taste
- 1 tablespoon olive oil
- 1/2 cup grated cheddar cheese

Method:

- Place a medium-sized skillet pan over medium heat, add oil and when heated, add onions.
- Let cook for 3 minutes or until tender.
- In the meantime, time, mash tofu until smooth.
- Add mashed tofu to the pan along with tomatoes and their juice and stir until well mixed.
- Then reduce heat to medium-low and season with salt, black pepper, and turmeric.

- Let cook for 2 to 3 minutes or until heated through, then sprinkle with cheese and serve.

Lunch

Roasted Brussels Sprouts with Parmesan Cheese

| Servings: 4 |
| Preparation time: 10 minutes | Cooking time: 20 minutes | Total time: 30 minutes |

Nutrition Value:
Calories: 236 Cal, Carbs: 14 g, Net Carbs: 8 g, Fat: 16 g, Protein: 13 g, Fiber: 6 g.

Ingredients:

- 20-ounce Brussels sprouts
- 1 teaspoon salt
- ½ teaspoon ground black pepper
- 1 teaspoon dried thyme
- 3 tablespoon olive oil
- 3-ounce grated parmesan cheese

Method:

- Set oven to 450 degrees F and let preheat.
- In the meantime, trim sprouts, then cut each in half and place in a baking dish.
- Drizzle with oil, then season with salt, black pepper, and thyme.
- Place baking dish into the oven and let cook for 15 to 20 minutes or until Brussels sprouts are nicely golden brown.
- When done, sprinkle with cheese and serve.

Dinner

Cilantro Lime Cauliflower Rice

| Servings: 5 |
| Preparation time: 10 minutes | Cooking time: 10 minutes | Total time: 20 minutes |

Nutrition Value:
Calories: 61 Cal, Carbs: 7 g, Net Carbs: 4 g, Fat: 5 g, Protein: 2.5 g, Fiber: 3 g.

Ingredients:

- 24-ounce head of cauliflower, riced
- 1/4 cup chopped cilantro
- 2 scallions, diced
- 1 tablespoon minced garlic
- 1 ½ teaspoon salt
- 1 teaspoon ground black pepper
- 1 tablespoon olive oil
- 1 1/2 limes, juiced

Method:

- Place a large skillet pan over medium heat, add oil and when heated, add scallions and garlic.
- Let cook for 3 to 4 minutes or until softened.
- Then turn heat to medium-high and add cauliflower rice.
- Stir until well mixed and let cook for 5 to 6 minutes or until cauliflower rice is tender-crisp.
- Season with salt and black pepper and transfer to serving platter.
- Drizzle with lime juice, sprinkle with cilantro and serve.

Day 25

Breakfast

Blueberries & Cream Crepes

| Servings: 2 |
| Preparation time: 10 minutes | Cooking time: 20 minutes | Total time: 30 minutes |

Nutrition Value:
Calories: 390 Cal, Carbs: 11 g, Net Carbs: 7 g, Fat: 32 g, Protein: 13 g, Fiber: 4 g.

Ingredients:

- 1/4 teaspoon baking soda
- 1/8 teaspoon sea salt
- 10 drops liquid stevia
- 1/4 teaspoon cinnamon
- 1 tablespoon coconut oil
- 2-ounce cream cheese
- 2 eggs

For Filling

- 60 grams blueberries
- 2 tablespoon erythritol, powdered
- 1/2 teaspoon vanilla extract, unsweetened
- 4-ounce cream cheese

Method:
- Crack eggs in a bowl, add cream cheese and beat using an electric hand immersion beater until smooth.
- Beat in salt, stevia, baking soda and cinnamon until combined.

- Place a pan over medium heat, add coconut oil and when heated, pour in ¼ cup of prepared batter.

- Then swirl the pan to spread and let cook for 3 minutes per side or until edges start to crisp.

- In the meantime, prepare filling by whisking together erythritol, vanilla and cream cheese using an electric hand immersion beater until creamy.

- Use remaining batter to cook more crepes, then spoon prepared filling in the center of each crepe, top with berries and wrap to serve.

Lunch

Caesar Salad

| Servings: 4 |
| Preparation time: 10 minutes | Cooking time: 0 minutes | Total time: 10 minutes |

Nutrition Value:
Calories: 168 Cal, Carbs: 11.1 g, Net Carbs: 5.2 g, Fat: 12.5 g, Protein: 6.6 g, Fiber: 5.9 g.

Ingredients:

- 1 medium avocado
- ¼ cup hemp seeds
- 12 cups chopped lettuce leaves
- 3 cup cherry tomatoes, halved
- 1 tablespoon capers
- 2 tablespoons minced garlic
- ½ teaspoon sea salt
- ½ teaspoon fresh ground pepper
- 2 teaspoons whole-grain mustard paste
- 1 tablespoon caper brine
- 3 tablespoons lemon juice
- 2 tablespoons water

Method:
- Peel and core avocado and add to food processor along with capers, garlic, salt, black pepper, mustard, capers brine, lemon juice, and water.
- Pulse at high speed for 1 to 2 minutes or until smooth and then tip this dressing in a bowl.
- Stir in hemp seeds until combined and add lettuce and tomatoes.

- Toss to coat and serve.

Dinner

Meatless Loaf

| Servings: 1 |
| Preparation time: 10 minutes | Cooking time: 45 minutes | Total time: 55 minutes |

Nutrition Value:
Calories: 125 Cal, Carbs: 10.2 g, Net Carbs: 6.2 g, Fat: 6.7 g, Protein: 10.4 g, Fiber: 4 g.

Ingredients:

- 12-ounce vegetarian burger crumbles
- 1/2 cup whole-grain bread crumbs
- ½ teaspoon garlic powder
- ¾ teaspoon salt
- ½ teaspoon ground black pepper
- 2 tablespoons onion dry soup mix
- 1 1/2 teaspoons olive oil
- 2 eggs, slightly beaten

Method:
- Set oven to 400 degrees F and let preheat.
- Place all the ingredients in a large bowl and stir until well mixed.
- Take a 9 by 5-inch loaf pan, grease inner side with oil and spoon prepared the batter in it.
- Spread and smooth top using a spatula and then place pan into the oven.
- Let bake for 30 to 45 minutes or until firm and cooked through.
- When done, take out meatloaf and slice to serve with salad.

Day 26

Breakfast

Chocolate Crunch Cereal

| Servings: 1 |
| Preparation time: 10 minutes | Cooking time: 25 minutes | Total time: 35 minutes |

Nutrition Value:
Calories: 400 Cal, Carbs: 12 g, Net Carbs: 7 g, Fat: 32 g, Protein: 15 g, Fiber: 5 g.

Ingredients:

- 2 tablespoons flaxseeds

- 1 tablespoon chia seeds

- ¾ tablespoon cocoa nibs, unsweetened

- 1/4 cup slivered almonds

- 1 tablespoon grated coconut, unsweetened

- 4 drops liquid stevia

- Almond milk as needed for serving, full-fat and unsweetened

Method:

- Place flaxseeds in a bowl and add chia seeds, cocoa, almond and coconut in it.

- Stir until mixed and then stir in stevia.

- Top with milk and serve.

Lunch

Caprese Grilled Eggplant Roll-Ups

| Servings: 8 |
| Preparation time: 5 minutes | Cooking time: 8 minutes | Total time: 13 minutes |

Nutrition Value:
Calories: 59 Cal, Carbs: 4 g, Net Carbs: 3 g, Fat: 3 g, Protein: 3 g, Fiber: 1 g.

Ingredients:

- 1 medium eggplant

- 1 large tomato

- 2 basil leaves, chopped

- Olive oil as needed

- 4-ounce mozzarella cheese

Method:

- Remove the stem of eggplant and cut into slices, each about 0.1 inch thick.

- Cut mozzarella cheese into thin slices along with tomatoes.

- Place a griddle pan over medium heat, grease with oil and let heat.

- In the meantime, brush oil on both sides of eggplant slices, then place onto heated griddle pan and let grill for 3 minutes per side.

- When both sides are a grill, top with a mozzarella slice, tomato slice and sprinkle with basil.

- Drizzle with oil, then sprinkle with black pepper and let cook for 1 minute or until liquid starts coming out of tomato slice.

- Transfer it to a clean working space and turn roll loosely and secure it with a toothpick.

- Prepare remaining rolls in the same manner and serve.

Dinner

Roasted Red Pepper Soup

| Servings: 4 |
| Preparation time: 10 minutes | Cooking time: 22 minutes | Total time: 32 minutes |

Nutrition Value:
Calories: 190.2 Cal, Carbs: 5.2 g, Net Carbs: 4.8 g, Fat: 16.4 g, Protein: 5.3 g, Fiber: 0.4 g.

Ingredients:

- 5 cups cauliflower florets

- ½ cup roasted red pepper, chopped

- 1 large white onion, peeled and finely chopped

- 1 teaspoon celery salt

- 1 tablespoon sea salt

- 1 teaspoon paprika, organic

- 1/8 teaspoon crushed red pepper flakes

- 1/8 teaspoon thyme

- 2 tablespoons coconut oil

- 1/8 teaspoon apple cider vinegar, organic

- 4 cups vegetable stock

- 1 cup coconut milk, full-fat and unsweetened

Method:
- Place a pot over medium heat, add oil and when heated, add onion.

- Let cook for 3 to 4 minutes or until softened and then stir in red pepper, celery salt, sea salt, paprika, red pepper flakes and thyme/

- Continue cooking for 3 minutes and then add remaining ingredients except for milk.

- Bring the mixture to simmer and let cook for 12 to 15 minutes or until florets are tender.

- Then remove the pot from heat and puree the soup using an electric hand immersion blender.

- Whisk in milk and serve.

Day 27

Breakfast

Pumpkin Maple Flaxseed Muffins

| Servings: 10 Muffins |
| Preparation time: 10 minutes | Cooking time: 20 minutes | Total time: 30 minutes |

Nutrition Value:
Calories: 120 Cal, Carbs: 2 g, Net Carbs: 1.2 g, Fat: 8.5 g, Protein: 5 g, Fiber: 0.8 g.

Ingredients:

- 1 1/4 cup flax seeds, ground
- 3 tablespoons pumpkin seeds
- 1/2 tablespoon baking powder
- 1/2 teaspoon salt
- 1/3 cup erythritol, granulated
- 1 tablespoon ground cinnamon
- 1 tablespoon pumpkin pie spice
- 1/4 cup erythritol, powdered
- 1/2 teaspoon apple cider vinegar, organic
- 1/2 teaspoon vanilla extract, unsweetened
- 1 egg
- 1 cup pure pumpkin puree
- 2 tablespoons coconut oil

Method:
- Set oven to 350 degrees F and let preheat.
- Ground flaxseeds in a food processor, then add to a bowl along with baking powder, salt, erythritol, cinnamon and pumpkin pie spice.

- Stir until just mixed and then stir in pumpkin puree until well combined.

- Stir in erythritol and vanilla extract.

- Crack an egg in it, add vinegar and mix until well combined.

- Line 10 cups in a muffin tray with muffin cups, then evenly divide prepared batter in it and top with pumpkin seeds.

- Place muffin tray into the oven and bake for 20 minutes or until muffins are nicely browned on top and inserted a skewer into each muffin comes out clean.

- When done, take out muffin cups and let cool slightly before serving.

Lunch

Tomato Soup

| Servings: 4 |
| Preparation time: 10 minutes | Cooking time: 5 minutes | Total time: 15 minutes |

Nutrition Value:
Calories: 460 Cal, Carbs: 16 g, Net Carbs: 8 g, Fat: 37.5 g, Protein: 11 g, Fiber: 8 g.

Ingredients:

- 4 tablespoons chopped green onion
- 1 tablespoon sea salt
- 2 teaspoons ground black pepper
- 2 teaspoon turmeric powder
- 1/4 cup red hot sauce, organic
- 1 teaspoon oregano
- 2 tablespoons apple cider vinegar, organic
- 1/4 cup olive oil
- 4 tablespoons coconut cream
- 4 tablespoons vegetarian butter
- 4 cups tomato soup

Method:

- Place all the ingredients in a large pot except for green onion and cream and stir until mixed.
- Place the pot over medium heat and let cook 5 minutes or until butter melts completely and soup comes to gentle boil.
- Then ladle soup into four serving bowl, top with green onions and coconut cream and serve.

Dinner

Spinach and Zucchini Lasagna

| Servings: 9 |
| Preparation time: 10 minutes | Cooking time: 1 hour | Total time: 1 hour and 10 minutes |

Nutrition Value:
Calories: 223 Cal, Carbs: 10.6 g, Net Carbs: 5.8 g, Fat: 12.4 g, Protein: 18.5 g, Fiber: 4.8 g.

Ingredients:

- 4 medium zucchinis
- 28-ounces tomatoes, peeled, cored and diced
- 3 cups baby spinach
- ½ of a medium white onion, peeled and chopped
- 4 teaspoons minced garlic
- 1 ½ teaspoon salt
- 1 teaspoon ground black pepper
- 1 tablespoon chopped basil
- 1/2 teaspoon parsley, chopped
- 2 tablespoons tomato paste
- 1 tablespoon olive oil
- 15-ounce ricotta cheese
- 16-ounces mozzarella cheese, grated
- 1 egg
- 1/2 cup grated Parmesan cheese

Method:

- Place a saucepan over medium heat, add oil and when heated, add onions.

- Let cook for 5 minutes or until soft and golden brown.

- Then stir in garlic and let cook for 1 minute or until fragrant.

- Stir tomatoes, salt, black pepper, and tomato paste and let cook for 25 to 30 minutes or until tomatoes are very tender, covering the pan.

- In the meantime, set the oven to 375 degrees F and let preheat.

- Cut zucchini into 1/8-inch slices and then arrange on a baking sheet in a single layer.

- Grease with oil, then place in oven, switch on the broiler and let broil for 6 to 8 minutes or until top is nicely golden brown.

- When done, remove baking sheet from oven, let zucchini rest for 5 minutes and then remove moisture from the sheet using paper towels, set aside.

- Place ricotta and parmesan cheese in a bowl, crack an egg in it and stir until well mixed.

- When tomatoes are cooked, stir in basil and spinach and taste to adjust seasoning.

- Take a by 12-inch casserole, spread prepared tomato-spinach mixture on the bottom, then cover with 5 to 6 slices of zucchini and spread with some of the prepared cheese mixture and sprinkle with some mozzarella cheese.

- Continue adding layers until all the ingredients are used and then cover casserole with aluminum foil.

- Place dish into the oven and let bake for 30 minutes.

- Then uncover dish and continue baking for another 10 minutes or until top is nicely golden brown.

- When done, let lasagna stand in a casserole for 10 minutes, then garnish with parsley and serve.

Breakfast

Grain-Free Granola

| Servings: 20 |
| Preparation time: 10 minutes | Cooking time: 25 minutes | Total time: 35 minutes |

Nutrition Value:
Calories: 529 Cal, Carbs: 6 g, Net Carbs: 1 g, Fat: 1 g, Protein: 1 g, Fiber: 0.7 g.

Ingredients:

- 1/3 cups sunflower seeds

- 1/3 cups pumpkin seeds

- 5 cups shredded coconut, unsweetened

- 1 cup almonds, chopped

- 1/4 cup cacao nibs, unsweetened

- 2 tablespoons orange zest

- 2 tablespoons erythritol, granulated

- 4 tablespoons cocoa powder, unsweetened

- 5 tablespoons coconut oil

Method:
- Place all the ingredients in a 6-quart slow cooker and stir until well mixed.

- Plug in the slow cooker, then cover with a lid and let cook for 2 hours at high heat setting or for 4 hours at low heating setting, stirring every 15 minutes at high or 30 minutes at low heat setting.

- Serve when ready.

Lunch

Creamy Cucumber & Dill Salad

| Servings: 6 |
| Preparation time: 10 minutes | Cooking time: 0 minutes | Total time: 10 minutes |

Nutrition Value:
Calories: 86 Cal, Carbs: 7 g, Net Carbs: 6 g, Fat: 1 g, Protein: 2 g, Fiber: 1 g.

Ingredients:

- 6 cups cucumber, peeled and chopped

- 2 tablespoons chopped dill

- 1 small red onion, peeled and thinly sliced

- ½ teaspoon garlic powder

- ½ teaspoon sea salt

- ¼ teaspoon black pepper

- 1 tablespoon olive oil

- 1 tablespoon lemon juice

- ½ cup sour cream, organic and full-fat

Method:

- Place all the ingredients except for cucumber and onions in a bowl and stir until well combined.

- Add cucumber and onions and toss to coat.

- Stir immediately.

Dinner

Zucchini Noodles with Avocado Sauce

| Servings: 2 |
| Preparation time: 15 minutes | Cooking time: 0 minutes | Total time: 15 minutes |

Nutrition Value:
Calories: 313 Cal, Carbs: 18.7 g, Net Carbs: 9 g, Fat: 26.8 g, Protein: 6.8 g, Fiber: 9.7 g.

Ingredients:

- 1 medium zucchini
- 1 medium avocado, pitted
- 12 cherry tomatoes, sliced
- 1 1/4 cup basil
- 1/3 cup water
- 4 tablespoons pine nuts
- 2 tablespoons lemon juice

Method:
- Rinse zucchini and then spiralized into thin noodles using noodle blade with spiralizer, set aside until required.
- Place all the ingredients except for tomatoes in a food processor and pulse at high speed or until smooth.
- Tip this sauce into a bowl, add zucchini noodles and tomato halves.
- Toss to coat and serve.

Breakfast

Almond Flour Biscuits

| Servings: 12 biscuits |
| Preparation time: 15 minutes | Cooking time: 15 minutes | Total time: 30 minutes |

Nutrition Value:
Calories: 164 Cal, Carbs: 4 g, Net Carbs: 2 g, Fat: 15 g, Protein: 5 g, Fiber: 2 g.

Ingredients:

- 2 cup almond flour
- 2 teaspoons baking powder
- 1/2 teaspoon sea salt
- 2 eggs, beaten
- 1/3 cup vegetarian butter

Method:
- Set oven to 350 degrees F and let preheat.
- Place flour in a bowl and stir in baking powder and salt until mixed.
- Crack eggs in it, add butter and whisk until well combined.
- Take a large baking sheet, line with parchment sheet and then place scoops of prepared batter using an ice cream scoop.
- Place the baking sheet into the oven and let bake for 15 minutes or until biscuits are nicely golden brown and firm.
- When done, let biscuits cool and then serve.

Lunch

Watermelon Pizza

| Servings: 8 slices |
| Preparation time: 10 minutes | Cooking time: 0 minutes | Total time: 10 minutes |

Nutrition Value:
Calories: 70 Cal, Carbs: 8 g, Net Carbs: 7 g, Fat: 4 g, Protein: 1 g, Fiber: 1 g.

Ingredients:

- 1 round slice of watermelon, about 1-inch thick
- 1/2 cup blueberries
- 1/2 cup raspberries
- 2 tablespoons erythritol, powdered
- 1/2 teaspoon vanilla extract, unsweetened
- 4 teaspoons lemon juice
- 3 tablespoons softened cream cheese, cubed
- 3 tablespoons whipping cream, organic and full-fat

Method:
- Place all the ingredients in a bowl except for watermelon and berries.
- Whisk until well combined and taste to adjust sweetness.
- Spread this mixture over watermelon slice and then scatter with berries.
- Slice to serve.

Dinner

Jalapeno Popper Cauliflower Casserole

| Servings: 6 |
| Preparation time: 10 minutes | Cooking time: 40 minutes | Total time: 50 minutes |

Nutrition Value:
Calories: 336 Cal, Carbs: 6.3 g, Net Carbs: 3.8 g, Fat: 29 g, Protein: 13 g, Fiber: 2.5 g.

Ingredients:

- 1 head of cauliflower, cut into florets
- ¼ cup and 1 tablespoon chopped jalapenos, seeds remove
- 1/4 teaspoon garlic powder
- 1 teaspoon salt
- ½ teaspoon ground black pepper
- 1/4 cup tomato salsa, fresh
- 2 tablespoons coconut cream, full-fat
- 1 tablespoon vegetarian butter
- 3/4 cup grated sharp cheddar cheese, shredded
- 3/4 cup shredded Colby jack cheese
- 1/2 cup shredded cheddar cheese
- 6-ounce cream cheese, softened

Method:

- Set oven to 375 degrees F and let preheat.
- Place cauliflower florets in a microwave proof bowl, stir in 1 tablespoon butter and 2 tablespoon coconut cream.
- Place bowl into the microwave and let microwave for 10 minutes at high heat setting.

- Then stir and puree mixture using an electric hand immersion blender.

- Add ¼ cup of cheddar cheese, 1 tablespoon jalapeño and garlic powder and puree again until smooth.

- Stir in salt and black pepper and set aside.

- Place cream cheese into a microwave ovenproof bowl and let microwave for 30 seconds at high heat setting or until softened.

- Then stir in ½ cup of cheddar cheese and salsa and mix until combined.

- Take a square baking dish, about 8 by 8 inches, and spread with prepared cauliflower puree.

- Layer with prepared cream cheese mixture and then scatter with jack cheese and remaining jalapeno pepper.

- Place baking dish into the oven and let bake for 20 minutes or until cheese melt completely.

- Then switch on the broiler and let broil for 6 to 8 minutes or until top is golden brown.

- Serve when done.

Breakfast

Cauliflower Hash Browns

| Servings: 4 |
| Preparation time: 5 minutes | Cooking time: 20 minutes | Total time: 25 minutes |

Nutrition Value:
Calories: 278 Cal, Carbs: 8 g, Net Carbs: 5 g, Fat: 26 g, Protein: 7 g, Fiber: 3 g.

Ingredients:

- 15-ounce head of cauliflower, riced

- 3 eggs

- ½ of a medium white onion, peeled and grated

- 1 teaspoon salt

- 1/8 teaspoon ground black pepper

- ½ cup olive oil

Method:
- Place cauliflower rice in a large bowl and add remaining ingredients.

- Stir until well combined and let rest for 10 minutes.

- When ready to cook, place a large pan over medium heat, and add oil and when heated, place scoops of prepared batter in a single layer, each 3-inch wide.

- Let fry for 4 to 5 minutes per side or until nicely golden brown.

- Prepare remaining hash browns in the same manner and serve.

Lunch

Creamy Snap Pea Radish Salad

| Servings: 4 cups |
| Preparation time: 10 minutes | Cooking time: 0 minutes | Total time: 10 minutes |

Nutrition Value:
Calories: 74 Cal, Carbs: 7 g, Net Carbs: 3 g, Fat: 4 g, Protein: 2 g, Fiber: 4 g.

Ingredients:

- 2 cups sugar snap peas, ends trimmed and halved
- 2 cups radish, peeled and sliced
- 2 medium cucumber, sliced

For Dressing

- 1 tablespoon chopped dill and more for garnishing
- 1 teaspoon garlic salt
- ¾ teaspoon ground black pepper
- 1 teaspoon apple cider vinegar, organic
- 1 teaspoon olive oil
- 1/4 cup sour cream organic and full-fat

Method:
- Place all the ingredients for dressing in a bowl and whisk until completely.
- Add radish, cucumber and snap peas and toss to coat.
- Taste to adjust seasoning, then garnishes with dill and serve.

Dinner

Zucchini & Sweet Potato Latkes

| Servings: 4 |
| Preparation time: 10 minutes | Cooking time: 8 minutes | Total time: 18 minutes |

Nutrition Value:
Calories: 122 Cal, Carbs: 7.95 g, Net Carbs: 6.25 g, Fat: 9 g, Protein: 3 g, Fiber: 1.7 g.

Ingredients:

- 1 cup grated zucchini

- 1 cup grated sweet potato

- ½ teaspoon garlic powder

- 1 teaspoon sea salt

- ½ teaspoon ground black pepper

- ¼ teaspoon ground cumin

- 1 tablespoon coconut flour

- ½ teaspoon dried parsley

- 2 tablespoons olive oil

- 1 egg, slightly beaten

Method:

- Place zucchini and sweet potato in a bowl.

- Crack an egg in it and whisk until combined.

- Place coconut flour in another bowl and stir in salt, black pepper, cumin, and parsley until mixed.

- Place a large pan over medium heat, add oil and when heated, drop prepared batter in four portions.

- Press each portion until ½-inch thick and let cook for 3 to 4 minutes per side or until nicely golden brown and crispy.

- When done, transfer latkes to a plate lined with paper towels and sprinkle with salt.

- Serve warm with salad.

Conclusion

The ketogenic diet is one of the trending diets to live a fit and long life. However, its macronutrients emphasis on the food with high-fat, moderate amount of protein and very less carb. Hence, this diet wasn't suitable for vegetarians. But, this versatile diet is favorable for meat lover as well as vegetarians.

The transition from a vegetarian to a Ketogenic vegetarian diet is easy. That individual would just have to keep close eyes on the carbs. But for a meat lover going to Ketogenic vegetarianism, this diet will be hard in the beginning.

This cookbook is written for both types of food lover to help with the overwhelming feeling when switching to this diet. With complete knowledge, food list and meal plan, this cookbook will give the confidence to get going with this diet. And the plus point, you will turn out an expert Keto vegetarian food expert.

Take a leap of faith and embrace this diet.

Manufactured by Amazon.ca
Bolton, ON

13832041R00092